MW00763660

Providence College
Providence, Rhode Island

Written by Kathryn Treadway

*Edited by Adam Burns, Meghan Dowdell,
Kimberly Moore, and Carrie Petersen*

Layout by Adam Burns

*Additional contributions by Omid Gohari,
Christina Koshzow, Chris Mason, Joey Rahimi,
and Luke Skurman*

ISBN # 1-4274-0114-4
ISSN # 1551-9937
© Copyright 2006 College Prowler
All Rights Reserved
Printed in the U.S.A.
www.collegeprowler.com

Last updated 5/13/06

Special Thanks To: Babs Carryer, Andy Hannah, LaunchCyte, Tim O'Brien, Bob Sehlinger, Thomas Emerson, Andrew Skurman, Barbara Skurman, Bert Mann, Dave Lehman, Daniel Fayock, Chris Babyak, The Donald H. Jones Center for Entrepreneurship, Terry Slease, Jerry McGinnis, Bill Ecenberger, Idie McGinty, Kyle Russell, Jacque Zaremba, Larry Winderbaum, Roland Allen, Jon Reider, Team Evankovich, Lauren Varacalli, Abu Noaman, Mark Exler, Daniel Steinmeyer, Jared Cohon, Gabriela Oates, David Koegler, Glen Meakem, and the Providence College Bounce-Back Team.

College Prowler®
5001 Baum Blvd.
Suite 750
Pittsburgh, PA 15213

Phone: 1-800-290-2682
Fax: 1-800-772-4972
E-Mail: info@collegeprowler.com
Web Site: www.collegeprowler.com

How this all started...

When I was trying to find the perfect college, I used every resource that was available to me. I went online to visit school websites; I talked with my high school guidance counselor; I read book after book; I hired a private counselor. Sure, this was all very helpful, but nothing really told me what life was like at the schools I cared about. These sources weren't giving me enough information to be totally confident in my decision.

In all my research, there were only two ways to get the information I wanted.

The first was to physically visit the campuses and see if things were really how the brochures described them, but this was quite expensive and not always feasible. The second involved a missing ingredient: the students. Actually talking to a few students at those schools gave me a taste of the information that I needed so badly. The problem was that I wanted more but didn't have access to enough people.

In the end, I weighed my options and decided on a school that felt right and had a great academic reputation, but truth be told, the choice was still very much a crapshoot. I had done as much research as any other student, but was I 100 percent positive that I had picked the school of my dreams?

Absolutely not.

My dream in creating *College Prowler* was to build a resource that people can use with confidence. My own college search experience taught me the importance of gaining true insider insight; that's why the majority of this guide is composed of quotes from actual students. After all, shouldn't you hear about a school from the people who know it best?

I hope you enjoy reading this book as much as I've enjoyed putting it together. Tell me what you think when you get a chance. I'd love to hear your college selection stories.

Luke Skurman
CEO and Co-Founder
lukeskurman@collegeprowler.com

Welcome to College Prowler®

During the writing of College Prowler's guidebooks, we felt it was critical that our content was unbiased and unaffiliated with any college or university. We think it's important that our readers get honest information and a realistic impression of the student opinions on any campus—that's why if any aspect of a particular school is terrible, we (unlike a campus brochure) intend to publish it. While we do keep an eye out for the occasional extremist—the cheerleader or the cynic—we take pride in letting the students tell it like it is. We strive to create a book that's as representative as possible of each particular campus. Our books cover both the good and the bad, and whether the survey responses point to recurring trends or a variation in opinion, these sentiments are directly and proportionally expressed through our guides.

College Prowler guidebooks are in the hands of students throughout the entire process of their creation. Because you can't make student-written guides without the students, we have students at each campus who help write, randomly survey their peers, edit, layout, and perform accuracy checks on every book that we publish. From the very beginning, student writers gather the most up-to-date stats, facts, and inside information on their colleges. They fill each section with student quotes and summarize the findings in editorial reviews. In addition, each school receives a collection of letter grades (A through F) that reflect student opinion and help to represent contentment, prominence, or satisfaction for each of our 20 specific categories. Just as in grade school, the higher the mark the more content, more prominent, or more satisfied the students are with the particular category.

Once a book is written, additional students serve as editors and check for accuracy even more extensively. Our bounce-back team—a group of randomly selected students who have no involvement with the project—are asked to read over the material in order to help ensure that the book accurately expresses every aspect of the university and its students. This same process is applied to the 200-plus schools College Prowler currently covers. Each book is the result of endless student contributions, hundreds of pages of research and writing, and countless hours of hard work. All of this has led to the creation of a student information network that stretches across the nation to every school that we cover. It's no easy accomplishment, but it's the reason that our guides are such a great resource.

When reading our books and looking at our grades, keep in mind that every college is different and that the students who make up each school are not uniform—as a result, it is important to assess schools on a case-by-case basis. Because it's impossible to summarize an entire school with a single number or description, each book provides a dialogue, not a decision, that's made up of 20 different topics and hundreds of student quotes. In the end, we hope that this guide will serve as a valuable tool in your college selection process. Enjoy!

OMID GOHARI ○ CHRISTINA KOSHZOW ○ CHRIS MASON ○ JOEY RAHIMI ○ LUKE SKURMAN ○
The College Prowler Team

Table of Contents

Introduction from the Author

A true story: while paying my bill for a diner, a heavily accented waiter approached the counter. Striking up a conversation, he inquired as to where I go to school. I confidently replied Providence College and smiled as I always do when I get to tell someone that I go to PC. The waiter nodded his approval, remarking, "Ah! A good, private institution," in an amusing way. As I returned to the table of my friends, I couldn't help smirking at the waiter's astute evaluation. PC is precisely that—a good, private institution.

Providence College boasts of a close-knit community of faculty and students located on historic Smith Hill in the city of Providence. Somehow, the school manages to enroll the most outgoing, giving, and intelligent young adults, and the results are well worth it. Providence students are eager to be involved, and the school prepares them to enter the world as informed, conscientious citizens. The Catholic Dominican tradition of the college works to develop PC alumni into virtuous models of civility with active concern for their community—both on a local and global level.

Unfamiliar to many outside the Northeast, if Providence is noticed, it is usually because of the Division I men's basketball team. PC offers much more than a fantastic sports program, and I hope that this guidebook assists you in discovering all PC has to extend to prospective students. Four years of your life will be spent at one college or another. The academics of all good schools basically averages out; you will get what you put in. Hopefully with this book, PC and its social atmosphere will come alive for you, making it that much easier to decide if Providence is what you're looking for, or if Providence is looking for you. You begin this book with the apropos closing words of Milton's *Paradise Lost*: "the world was all before them, where to choose their place of rest, and Providence their guide . . ."

Kathryn Treadway, Author
Providence College

By the Numbers

General Information

Providence College
549 River Avenue
Providence, RI 02918

Control:
Private

Academic Calendar:
Semester

Religious Affiliation:
Roman Catholic

Founded:
1917

Web Site:
www.providence.edu

Main Phone:
(401) 865-2000

Admissions Phone:
(401) 865-2535

Student Body

**Full-Time
Undergraduates:**
3,822

**Part-Time
Undergraduates:**
666

**Total Male
Undergraduates:**
1,915

**Total Female
Undergraduates:**
2,573

Admissions

Overall Acceptance Rate:
54%

Regular Acceptance Rate:
54%

Total Applicants:
7,824

Total Acceptances:
4,204

Freshman Enrollment:
1,037

Yield (% of admitted students who actually enroll):
25%

Early Decision Available?
No

Early Action Available?
Yes

Early Action Acceptance Rate:
63%

Early Action Deadline:
November 1

Regular Decision Deadline:
January 15

Regular Decision Notification:
April 1

Must Reply-By Date:
May 1

Applicants Placed on Waiting List:
1,526

Applicants Accepted From Waiting List:
702

Applicants Enrolled From Waiting List:
221

Transfer Applications Received:
232

Transfer Applications Accepted:
92

Transfer Students Enrolled:
67

Transfer Applicant Acceptance Rate:
40%

Common Application Accepted?
Yes, with supplemental forms

Admissions E-Mail:
pcadmiss@providence.edu

Admissions Web Site:
www.providence.edu/ admissions

SAT I or ACT Required?
Either

**SAT I Range
(25th–75th Percentile):**
1110–1290

**SAT I Verbal Range
(25th–75th Percentile):**
550–640

**SAT I Math Range
(25th–75th Percentile):**
560–650

SAT II Requirements:
None

Retention Rate:
92%

**Top 10% of High
School Class:**
42%

Application Fee:
$55

Financial Information

Full-Time Tuition:
$25,310

Room and Board:
$9,270

Books and Supplies:
$750

**Average Need-Based
Financial Aid Package
(including loans, work-study,
grants, and other sources):**
$14,800

**Students Who Applied
For Financial Aid:**
69%

Students Who Received Aid:
62%

Financial Aid Forms Deadline:
February 1

Financial Aid Phone:
(401) 865-2286

Financial Aid E-Mail:
finaid@providence.edu

Financial Aid Web Site:
*www.providence.edu/
Admission/Undergraduate+
Financial+Aid*

Academics

The Lowdown On...
Academics

Degrees Awarded:
Associate
Bachelor
Master

Most Popular Majors:
30% Business Management,
    Marketing
14% Social Sciences
11% Education
 8% English Language,
    Literature
 7% History

Full-Time Faculty:
262

**Faculty with
Terminal Degree:**
88%

**Student-to-Faculty
Ratio:**
13:1

Average Course Load:
15 Credits (or 5 classes)

Graduation Rates:
Four-Year: 82%
Five-Year: 84%
Six-Year: 85%

Special Degree Options
Accelerated masters programs: optometry, BS/BA/MBA
Intercollege Programs: 3-2 engineering/physics systems with
Colombia University and Washington University in St. Louis

AP Test Score Requirements
Possible credit for scores of 4 or 5

IB Test Score Requirements
Used for placement only

Sample Academic Clubs
Alpha Delta Mu, Alpha Epsilon Delta, Amigos Unidos, Circolo
Italiano, Gamma Kappa Alpha, Law Society, National Society
of Collegiate Scholars, Philosophy Club

Did You Know?

Just feel like skipping Development of Western Civilization class? No problem! **Audio tapes of Civ lectures are available** for students to listen to, whether you missed class or just want to make sure you got that date right for the next quiz.

There is **no such thing as a teacher's assistant** teaching a class at Providence College.

Midnight the night before finals begin, underclassmen gather on the quad to **release some of the stress of finals** at the annual "Civ Scream." Amidst the streakers, water balloons, and Red Bull, you can hear the cry, "Civ Sucks!"

Best Places to Study:

Aquinas Lounge, Library, St. Dominic's Chapel, Slavin Center

Students Speak Out On...
Academics

"Most professors at PC make a sincere effort to get to know their students personally. The small class sizes make this possible and create an excellent atmosphere for open class discussions. You can tell the professors love their jobs."

Q "**Professors are here for students 100 percent**. I can't think of a time where a professor was not willing to help with something. Plus, they're able to hook you up with tutors if you need even more help with a classroom assignment."

Q "Some teachers are wonderful, enthusiastic, and completely interesting, while others can be ridiculously **boring and hard to stay awake for**. Sometimes, it's luck of the draw when you sign up for a class and don't know the teacher."

Q "The professors are usually incredibly friendly and helpful. Many of them take an active interest in student life. I have seen **professors show up to their students' athletic games** and send out mass e-mails encouraging other students to also attend."

Q "I have found that all of my professors have been very passionate about their subject and also **make themselves very accessible to the students**. PC's academic setting can be a very advantageous environment to the undeclared student, as it is very encouraging of students to test the waters to discover subject matter that interests them before committing to a major."

Q "The Providence College faculty is made up of professors who have the **highest degrees attainable in their particular fields**. This definitely shows you that they are extremely qualified to teach the subjects that they do. Despite this fact, some particular professors are not great teachers; they lack personality, the ability to interact with students and even other faculty members, which makes the learning experience quite dull and uninspiring. But a vast majority of the professors I have had thus far have been great."

Q "One of the best things about professors at PC is the fact that they're always accessible. They make it easy to contact them, **often giving you their home phone numbers**. I'd say that most of the classes are interesting, but I have to admit a professor can make or break the class."

Q "I feel the teachers can be **anywhere from fairly liberal to extremely conservative**. I guess you can't expect too much from a Catholic school. Some teachers are cold, boring, and confusing, while others can be extremely interesting and fun."

Q "I have encountered very few professors, if any for that matter, that have not been **willing to go the extra mile** and help me improve their class."

Q "**Students take an active role in their education** rather than a professor lecturing the entire class."

Q "I've found that the **classes involved in my major are the most interesting to me**. Some of the core classes that I've had to take have been less interesting to me."

Q "Classes within my major **I find particularly interesting**, especially as I have advanced into seminars."

The College Prowler Take On...
Academics

The students of Providence College have developed spilt personality disorders. Let me clarify: Monday through Friday, earnest, eager-to-learn scholars diligently devote themselves to edifying endeavors. Then, with dismissal from their last class of the week, a Jekyll and Hyde transformation occurs. Students who study hard during the week and party harder during the weekend matriculate PC. Professors at PC, although varying in teaching style, all possess a genuine concern for their students, often going above and beyond the average to make themselves accessible. Like all colleges, professors and their classes cover the entire spectrum, from liberal and eccentric, to conservative and traditional.

While most major courses are stimulating, core classes can be tedious and downright painful. A unique and central experience for the PC student is the Development of Western Civilization course (Civ). Requiring you to attend class five days a week for four consecutive semesters can seem, at first, a legal means of torture that somehow slipped past the founding fathers when drafting the Bill of Rights. The program is not some remnant of medieval torture passed down in the Dominican tradition since the time of St. Thomas Aquinas, but a comprehensive examination of Western civilization since its dawn in Mesopotamia a millennia ago continuing into the modern age. Civ not only gives PC students the thread to unravel the tapestry of civilization, but also allows them to view the weaving of at least four disciplines (literature, history, philosophy, and theology) into one course, an impressive undertaking not available at most colleges. Although Civ may be a challenge, it is one every PCer is proud to have completed. It remains a core class whose legacy continues long after you are "done with Civ." Another boon of Providence academics is the notable lack of teaching assistants. A professor teaches every class, and students will find competing with difficult accents to be nearly nonexistent.

B

The College Prowler® Grade on
Academics: B

A high Academics grade generally indicates that professors are knowledgeable, accessible, and genuinely interested in their students' welfare. Other determining factors include class size, how well professors communicate, and whether or not classes are engaging.

Local Atmosphere

The Lowdown On...
Local Atmosphere

Region:
Northeast

City, State:
Providence, RI

Setting:
Medium-sized city

Distance from New York:
3 hours

Distance from Boston:
1 hour

Points of Interest:
Fleet Skating Center
Providence Place Mall
Roger Williams Park Botanical Gardens
Roger Williams Park Zoo
Thayer Street
WaterFire

Closest Movie Theaters:

Avon Cinema

260 Thayer Street

(401) 421-3315

Feinstein IMAX Theatre

9 Providence Place

(401) 453-IMAX

National Amusements
Cinema 16

Providence Place Mall

(401) 270-4646

Closest Shopping Malls:

Providence Place Mall

Thayer Street

White City Shopping Center

Major Sports Teams:

Boston Bruins (hockey)

Boston Red Sox (baseball)

New England Patriots
(football)

City Web Sites

www.providenceri.com

www.jumptoprovidence.com

Did You Know?

5 Fun Facts about Providence:

- Providence is **known as the Renaissance City**.

- The plans drawn up by the architects of the State House originally called for a female figure to sit atop the dome. The **Independence Man** now residing there is 11 feet tall and stands 278 feet off the ground.

- In *Amistad*, the Rhode Island State House was depicted as the U.S. Capitol building. *There's Something About Mary*, *Outside Providence*, and **NBC's TV show, *Providence***, also utilized the city during filming.

- A state referendum **exempts artists** living in Downcity (downtown) from state income taxes.

- The Dunkin' Donuts Center (the Dunk) is an indoor sports and entertainment venue that **seats 14,500 people and is home to PC's men's basketball team**, as well as the Providence Bruins.

Famous People from Providence:

George M. Cohan – America's first acting superstar

Nelson Eddy – Actor, singer

Bobby Hackett – Jazz artist

Ruth Hussey – Actress

Galway Kinnell – Poet

H.P. Lovecraft – Fiction writer

Local Slang:

Bubbler – What a Providence native calls a water fountain.

Sub – A hot sandwich known elsewhere as a hero.

Wicked – An adjective used instead of the word very.

Students Speak Out On...
Local Atmosphere

"**The atmosphere of Smith Hill sharply contrasts with that of the one inside the 'PC Bubble.' Surrounding the $30,000-a-year college is a neighborhood abundant with poverty and several low-income housing projects.**"

Q "Often, students are alerted of crimes and assaults occurring right outside the campus walls and sometimes even inside. Johnson & Wales University and Rhode Island College are **some other universities within a mile of PC**. A popular place for many PC students is right up the road at Providence Place Mall and Federal Hill."

Q "The immediate area is up-and-coming, due largely in part to the community service of PC students. Downtown, there are tons of things to do. The mall is new; Thayer Street is kind of an eclectic shopping and eating district; the beaches like Narragansett and Newport are within 45 minutes of campus. Basically, **anything and everything that you could want** to do in a city is here. There are four additional colleges in Providence-Brown University, Johnson & Wales University, Rhode Island College, and Rhode Island School of Design. PC students don't tend to really hang around with these other schools, though; we're pretty much a self-contained campus."

Q "Providence is a wonderful city with so much to do: shopping, eating, and theater. The one thing to stay away from is some of the **scary streets that directly surround campus**. It's not the safest ever."

Q "**The city of Providence is truly a Renaissance city**. In recent years, there has been much improvement to the city that has made it a beautiful, fun, wonderful place to attend college. There are bars, clubs, movies, coffee shops, and during the warmer months, the city lights up the river in an event called WaterFire. Unfortunately, PC is not in the greatest area of Providence, so one must use caution and common sense when walking at night. However, I have not felt uncomfortable yet."

Q "Being a New England city, **Providence is rich in history and culture**, so there are many attractions for its residents; but in any city, there are plenty of places that are dangerous and should be avoided, and Providence has its share."

Q "Providence is known as a city that is up-and-coming. PC is a school whose **campus promotes a close-knit, welcoming environment**, yet at the same time, Providence College students have all the advantages of living in a large city that offers many cultural and entertainment opportunities."

Q "I love the atmosphere in Providence. While there are other colleges around, **PC students tend to stick together**, for the most part, at the same off-campus areas. This establishes a familiarity within the student body."

Q "Personally, I really enjoy Providence. **It's compact enough so that I can easily ride my bike** to most places I need to go, but big enough to offer me opportunities for entertainment and growth outside of PC."

Q "Providence College is right in the middle of a lower-class neighborhood. Part of the surrounding area is not too nice. However, once you get downtown (which is not far at all), it is a lot nicer, and **there are some fun things to do**. There are some cool music venues if you're into that sort of thing. I really enjoy going to Lupo's for small but great shows."

Q "Providence is wonderful! A student receives all the benefits of a city atmosphere while **also feeling as if they are living in a suburb**. There are several other colleges and universities in the area and lots of places to visit; you have Thayer Street, you can see a show at PPAC, and you can see a concert at the Dunkin' Donuts Center. There are museums, not to mention adorable coffee houses and restaurants."

Q "One of the organizations on campus (the Board of Programmers) will **bring students to tons of places—** Fenway, New York, and the Providence Performing Arts Center."

The College Prowler Take On...
Local Atmosphere

Pop! You have stepped off Huxley Avenue, popping the "PC Bubble." The small, private, Catholic campus is precariously encircled by poverty-stricken North Providence. While the area directly surrounding campus is one that anyone with presence of mind avoids, PC is minutes away from downtown Providence. The heart of this cleaner, smaller version of Boston is home to numerous hot spots for college students. The new Providence Place Mall is five floors of carpeted consumer bliss, and it houses such eateries as the Cheesecake Factory, Joe's American Bar and Grille, Napa Valley, and Uno's. An eclectic mix of shops and restaurants can be found on Thayer Street, near Brown University. With numerous entertainment venues from the Providence Performing Arts Center to the Dunkin' Donuts Center, Providence has something for everyone.

Providence College has all the benefits of a small, close-knit school in an urban setting. For those who do not enjoy the drinking scene, there are countless options to keep you busy around town. Because of the poor area in the vicinity of the school, walking places is not the best idea, but biking, cabs, and free RIPTA buses are always an option. Overall, Providence is a city irradiating a vivacity and youthfulness that can only be attributed to the several nearby colleges and universities.

B+

The College Prowler® Grade on
Local Atmosphere: B+

A high Local Atmosphere grade indicates that the area surrounding campus is safe and scenic. Other factors include nearby attractions, proximity to other schools, and the town's attitude toward students.

Safety & Security

The Lowdown On...
Safety & Security

Number of PC Police:
32

PC Police Phone:
Non-emergencies
(401) 865-2391

Emergencies
(401) 865-2222

Safety Services:
24-hour foot and
vehicle patrols

Controlled dormitory access

Emergency phones

Late-night shuttle and
escort services

Lighted pathways
and sidewalks

Rape defense classes (RAD)

Student patrols

Health Services:
Basic medical services

Gynecological clinic

Health Center Office Hours:

Monday–Friday 8:30 a.m.–4:30 p.m.
Gynecological Clinic: Tuesday (by appointment only)
EMT: Monday–Friday 4:30 p.m.–8:30 a.m.

Did You Know?

The Health Center has a **doctor available at 9 a.m. Monday through Friday**. The Personal Counseling Center works in cooperation with Health Services for counseling and psychological services.

Students Speak Out On...
Safety & Security

"PC tries to provide students with the best security possible. The three all-female dorms have night guards that stay at the entrances. Three security stations at the River Avenue, Huxley Avenue, and Eaton Street entrances monitor incoming guests."

Q "Sometimes, PC students will mock PC security, but there was **never a time that I felt unsafe** as a student on the PC campus."

Q "Basically, **security is tight**, but it's still important to use street smarts on campus—walk in groups especially, at night, don't make yourself a target for crime by flashing expensive electronic equipment, and take advantage of the security features provided by the College."

Q "Security is stupid; **anyone and everyone can get onto campus** and in and out the dorms very easily. It's nice not to have to worry about any sort of hassle getting friends from outside of school onto campus, but it's scary to think of all the things that could happen due to lack of security."

Q "The **security on campus, to be honest, is worthless**. Men in their 90s aren't my idea of adequate security. Dunbar is the only useful security guard we have."

Q "Security and safety at school is something that, in my three years thus far, I am aware they have tried to beef up; yet, **there is still a lot of work needed to be done**."

Q "Safety on campus is totally blown out of proportion. Many people cite the neighborhood as a problem and think the residents are willing to come on to campus to harm unsuspecting college students, which is definitely not the case. Campus is quite safe, and **security does a good job in maintaining this safety**. I feel that many students might feel unsafe at times because they are unfamiliar with the neighborhood, and the neighborhood is unfamiliar with them."

Q "Providence College is a very safe campus. However, once you get off campus, it can be unsafe at times. There are **muggings and assaults** on the nearby streets."

Q "The general area surrounding PC has improved over the past year with the addition of a police substation right down the street from the school. Like always, **students should use caution when walking at night** and when walking alone, as well. The security department does a very decent job of keeping the campus safe and secure."

The College Prowler Take On...
Safety & Security

Ah! The age-old question that haunts parents of college-bound children: is my child going to be safe at school? Providence College takes safety and security seriously, as the numerous lectures on it during orientation and freshman year prove. While freshman girls may feel like living in an all-girl dorm, which requires males to sign in, is like living in a prison, others consider the Huxley Avenue entrance a security joke. Overall, PC has put into place numerous security measures to ensure both student and parental peace of mind. The use of common sense and awareness of one's surroundings is the best preventative measure. General consensus relates, "I have never felt unsafe at PC."

Operating on the blue-light system, PC has emergency call-boxes all over campus. Escort and shuttle services are available, and the all-female dorms are monitored by guards. While getting on to campus is simple, the real safety of students is up to themselves—that is why we are constantly reminded not to let anyone we do not know into the card-controlled dorms. PC security can boast of a fantastic reaction time and personal concern for the students. The administration excels in keeping students informed by posting occurrences and security concerns.

B-

The College Prowler® Grade on
Safety &
Security: B-

A high grade in Safety & Security means that students generally feel safe, campus police are visible, blue-light phones and escort services are readily available, and safety precautions are not overly necessary.

Computers

The Lowdown On...
Computers

High-Speed Network?
Yes

Operating Systems:
PC, Mac, and UNIX

Wireless Network?
Yes

24-Hour Labs:
None

Number of Labs:
8

Charge to Print?
No

Number of Computers:
150

Discounted Software

None

Free Software

None

Did You Know?

Laptops are available for checkout at the circulations desk in the library for a two-hour period of use.

Students Speak Out On...
Computers

"There may be a few days of downtime throughout the year, but for the most part, you can be online all the time—which is both a blessing and a curse because you may become addicted to AIM!"

Q "There are **eight computer labs on campus**; it's usually never hard to find a computer if need be. I find that most students have their own computer, but a lot of times, it's for more personal use. I would recommend having one. It's simply fun."

Q "The **computer service in the labs is excellent**, though they always seem to be the most crowded when you need them most. As for the individual rooms, the Internet service is severely inept."

Q "I must say that the Providence College network is one of the worst you can ever find. It is **slow, always littered with countless viruses**, and not on the cutting edge of technology. Most computer labs can get fairly crowded, but it depends on location, time of day, and time of year."

Q "There are plenty of computer labs on campus in the various buildings, and while **during midterm and final weeks they tend to be in higher demand**, there is still availability as long as one can be flexible."

Q "The **computer labs aren't usually very crowded**, and the network usually runs pretty well. But, I recommend that every student bring his/her own computer."

Q "Generally speaking, there are plenty of computers available, but not bringing a computer is a big risk to take, **especially around finals time**. I frequently make use of the printers in the library. All of the course registration is done online, so it goes very quickly, but there are often errors and delays in the system due to the high number of students accessing the network at once. On those days, the computer labs flooded with students."

Q "The network is usually good, but **sometimes, is a bit slow**. When it comes to registration, it gets a little out of whack, which can be frustrating."

Q "The **computer labs are usually easy to use**; it's only overcrowded during exam periods. A computer is definitely not needed academically, but for personal and social reasons, I definitely would recommend it."

Q "**The computer network is inconsistent**. At times, it can be very fast and helpful, but other times, it can be slow and a burden."

Q "**To have your own computer on campus is certainly a luxury and a privilege** that most students have. The computer network is good. You can do everything from submit postings about your class on the Angel network to check what the balance is on your tuition on Cyberfriar. Sometimes, with the frequent use of Instant Messenger, the network becomes slow."

The College Prowler Take On...
Computers

At least thrice a year you will get an e-mail explaining that the network will be shut down for a period of about four hours due to servicing. It's hard to maintain control of your emotions when you receive such news. What on earth will you do without AIM for four hours? The answer comes, a lightning flash of insight: Snood. Those two activities are the real reason you'll want to bring your own computer to PC. The computer labs on campus are sufficient but can get crowded during midterms and finals. If you are able to employ a degree of leniency into your schedule, you will be fine. The network at PC is comparative to high-speed DSL and more importantly, it's free, which is music to a college student's ears. The degree of felicity supplied by the network varies from frustration to complete satisfaction.

The network has its ups and downs throughout the year. Students are responsible for their own virus software, which, if everyone used, would seriously diminish the viruses on the network and increase server speed. The Help Desk and Computer Services are always willing to help if you do get a virus or just have a persnickety laptop. It is important, if you bring a computer to school, to purchase virus software and a lock to secure your laptop to the desk. While theft is not a frequent occurrence on campus, you want to take every precaution available, including registering high-priced equipment with the Office of Safety and Security. As a matter of convenience and social utility, your own computer is the best route to go. Besides, who wants to actually call people to make plans for dinner when you can instant message all 20 of them at once?

The College Prowler® Grade on

Computers: B-

A high grade in Computers designates that computer labs are available, the computer network is easily accessible, and the campus' computing technology is up-to-date.

Facilities

The Lowdown On...
Facilities

Student Center:
Slavin Center

Athletic Center:
Peterson Recreation Center

Libraries:
Phillips Memorial

Campus Size:
105 acres

Popular Places to Chill:
Alumni Hall Cafeteria
McPhails
The quad

What Is There to Do on Campus?

Find yourself with time to spare between classes? No problem. Try hitting up the gym, tossing a Frisbee on the quad, popping in at the Fine Arts Center to see student work or grab some popcorn and a milkshake in McPhails.

Movie Theater on Campus?

No, but there are outdoor movies on Slavin lawn occasionally.

Bowling on Campus?

No

Bar on Campus?

McPhails

Coffeehouse on Campus?

No

Favorite Things to Do

The artistically inclined can check out the latest student masterpieces at the Hunt-Cavanaugh Gallery, as well as the new Smith Center for the Fine Arts. The Guzman Chapel holds performances by the musically gifted students of PC. Blackfriars Theater hosts the school's dramatic productions twice a year. Board of Programmers and the SAIL office offer numerous entertainment events, including concerts twice a year (by bands like the Roots), karaoke in McPhails, and even a hypnotist in '64 Hall. But many students' thing to do is to catch a show by Rejects on the Rise, PC's very own improv group—if you want to laugh really hard, be sure to check them out.

Students Speak Out On...
Facilities

"PC is just finishing a restoration and renovation period, so many of the facilities on campus are changing for the better. The library looks brand new and has just added state-of-the-art computers."

Q "The **student center and the computer labs are nice**, not spectacular like you see at big state universities, but appropriate for our small, close-knit student body."

Q "The athletic facilities are sometimes too crowded, and **the weight room is extremely small**. As a Big East school, I had expected larger facilities and better equipment."

Q "The **facilities are nice**, open areas. Especially with the recent addition of McPhails on our campus, it invites and accommodates more on-campus activity among students."

Q "For anyone who is looking at PC now, the facilities are state-of-the-art. There are several buildings which needed updating when I looked at PC, but **they are in the middle of a lot of renovations**, which have made the campus almost brand new."

Q "They're alright; when I first visited the school, I really **didn't think anything special of its appearance**. For one, we're not big on grass. But again, the people and the spirit make that almost unnoticeable."

Q "The **athletic center isn't that great**. Sometimes, you just want to go play basketball, and you can't because they are using the courts for some other activity. They are in desperate need of a new athletic facility. The computers in the labs are pretty good. The student center is very nice. We recently had a new campus bar and hangout built; it's a good place to go play pool, ping pong, or watch a baseball game on the big screen television."

Q "PC's athletic facility is under **new additions of turf fields, aerobic rooms**, and hopefully in a few years, an outdoor track. Overall, the athletic department is budgeting multi-millions from fund-raising for all the new updates. Some athletic facilities, such as Peterson, are only accessible to non-athletes, so that the facility is not occupied by varsity athletes."

The College Prowler Take On...
Facilities

Every year seems to be a year of renewal for Providence College. Returning students to the PC campus eagerly anticipate new structures and edifices upon return each September. While having grown accustomed to the new restaurant-style look of Raymond Dining Hall, an addition to the dining hall was added in 2004. In 2005, the interior of the Smith Center for the Fine Arts was erected, students arrived to find a masterpiece that hopefully will originate many other masterpieces within its walls. The suites will be completed soon, and the quad they have created on lower campus is going to be a hot spot among students and tourists alike. A turf field will also hide an underground parking field. Athletically-inclined students were ecstatic as the school announced renovations on the Nautilus weight room and the addition of a glass-enclosed room to Peterson.

With so many construction projects nearing completion the Providence campus will have an entirely new look for returning students and fantastic new facilities for the incoming class to utilize. Providence administration deserves a round of applause for addressing the needs of the student body in building and refurbishing the campus in so short a period of time. The campus will now be filled with the hustle and bustle of merry students rather than scaffolding, workmen, and the melody of heavy machinery.

B

The College Prowler® Grade on

Facilities: B

A high Facilities grade indicates that the campus is aesthetically pleasing and well-maintained; facilities are state-of-the-art, and libraries are exceptional. Other determining factors include the quality of both athletic and student centers and an abundance of things to do on campus.

Campus Dining

The Lowdown On...
Campus Dining

Freshman Meal Plan Requirement?
Yes

Meal Plan Average Cost:
$1,925 per semester
(19 meals per week)

Places to Grab a Bite with Your Meal Plan:

Alumni Hall Food Court
Food: Deli, grill, entree, international, pizza, bakery, deli, coffee, desserts
Location: Slavin Center
Hours: Monday–Thursday 7:30 a.m.–12 a.m., Friday 7:30 a.m.– 1 a.m., Saturday 12 p.m.–1 a.m., Sunday 12 p.m.–12 a.m.

Raymond Dining Hall

Food: Classics, theme cuisine, pizza, deli, grill, ice cream, box lunches to go

Location: South Campus

Hours: Monday–Thursday 7:30 a.m.–10:30 a.m., 11 a.m.–2 p.m., 11 a.m.– 3 p.m., 4:30 p.m.–8 p.m., Friday 7:30 a.m.–10:30 a.m., 11 a.m.–2 p.m., 11 a.m.– 3 p.m., 4:30 p.m.–6:30 p.m.

Box meals: Monday–Friday 7:30 a.m.–3 p.m.

Saturday–Sunday 9 a.m.– 1:45 p.m., 4 p.m.–6:30 p.m.

Off-Campus Places to Use Your Meal Plan:

None

24-Hour On-Campus Eating?

None

Student Favorites:

The Grill, Theme Cuisine, and Pizzeria stations in Raymond Dining Hall

Did You Know?

Some dorms have a kitchen if you're feeling up to the task of a home-cooked meal.

Students Speak Out On...
Campus Dining

> **"The main cafeteria, Raymond Hall, tries to vary the meal choices, and towards the end of the year, they were getting better at providing more choices of protein and vegetables."**

Q "I actually don't mind the dining hall. Just like any college, the **food can be a little repetitive**, but it's pretty good."

Q "**Raymond Hall is our main dining facility on campus**. You can get almost anything you want to eat, and it's open most of the day. The favorite meal of the week tends to be weekend brunch."

Q "Raymond Hall—eh, I've had better college food. But the good news is you can always find something to eat. But **'Ray' is a great place to socialize**! And it's all-you-can-eat and has good desserts. Oh yeah, and the staff is awesome! Slavin is much better food than Ray and a little more expensive. It's a debit system. It's a great place to grab a snack at night or to meet with a study group."

Q "Food is not that great on campus, but **it is not that bad**. Most people decide to eat off campus or order out to avoid the monotony of the dishes served at school. It would be nice to actually have a restaurant on campus like I know other schools do."

Q "**It's all run by Sodexho**, who serves 90 percent of the schools in the U.S., so it's going to be about the same wherever you go."

Q "The food is getting better every year I return to campus. **The dining company has a wide variety of foods** to choose from, and they've started to become more health conscious about what meals they are giving PC students."

Q "The main dining hall always provides ample, good food so long as one remains creative. While courses may repeat themselves over the month, **a student can mix and match from all different food stations** and become his own chef. It would be great to get a coffee shop on campus."

Q "The food on campus is pretty good, not as good as home cooking, **but good for college food**. They have a huge variety, and personally, being a vegetarian, they offered a lot of choices for me."

Q "The food on campus is not going to be your mom's home-cooked meal, but **Raymond Cafeteria does it for me the majority of the time**. The best part about the cafeteria is the new restaurant-style booths, which give a sense of privacy when you're there with a group of friends."

Q "For second semester, I endured the sandwich line because **I could not deal anymore with the hot food** and crappy salad bar. The food is the one thing I'm not looking forward to going back to. It's fine if you don't have to be diet conscious, but Ray will add more onto the Freshman 15 than the local bars will."

The College Prowler Take On...
Campus Dining

There are two sources of food on campus: Raymond Dining Hall and Alumni Food Court in the Slavin Center. Ray Café, the main cafeteria at PC and the one at which your meal plan applies, was refurbished in 2003. Although the decor was jazzed up with the addition of booths, swank lighting, and iron grating for the individual stations, Ray can leave a bitter taste in the mouth of some of PC's more finicky eaters. With new interior design comes a new menu—a more diverse one at that. Items such as rosemary chicken and falafel bars now mingle among the staples of burgers (both the meat and vegetable variety), fries, and the salad bar. Slavin is the epitome of fine dining on the PC campus. Slay, as it is affectionately termed, carries something for everyone. Whether it's a burger off "the Grill", chicken parm from the "the Pizzeria," or a fresh sandwich from "the Deli," there is always an option when Ray is extra disappointing.

Ray may not be the equivalent of a home-cooked meal, but its yum factor is increased exponentially by the Ray staff, who are the most darling women you have ever met. Those lacking an iron stomach and the courage needed to attempt the more exotic cuisine can take solace; Ray Café is the best place to eat when they keep it simple and stick to the basics. Slavin is the place to be if you have a group project or can tolerate noise and interruptions when you are studying. The drawback (other than the ridiculously overpriced salad bar) is that Slavin requires money that is put on your all-purpose Providence College ID card at the start of every semester. The amount depends on your meal plan, and generally, the fewer meals you have at Ray, the more "Slavinbucks" you get. Regardless of the amount you have in the beginning, your funds will diminish rapidly as the semester progresses, until you are left with that random 23 cents that won't buy anything. You or your parents can always add more money to your card, and there is always the option of paying in cash.

The College Prowler® Grade on
Campus Dining: C+

Our grade on Campus Dining addresses the quality of both school-owned dining halls and independent on-campus restaurants as well as the price, availability, and variety of food.

Off-Campus Dining

The Lowdown On...
Off-Campus Dining

Restaurant Prowler:
Popular Places to Eat!

Admiral Spa Inc.
Food: Breakfast
680 Admiral St.
(401) 831-5178
Cool Features: Great breakfast food for drunk students
Price: $9 and under per person
Hours: Daily 5 a.m.–2 p.m.

Antonio's Pizza
Food: Pizza
258 Thayer St.
(401) 455-3600
Cool Features: Gourmet pizza
Price: $15 and under per person
Hours: Monday–Wednesday 11 a.m.–1:30 a.m., Thursday–Saturday 11 a.m.–2 a.m.

→

Blue Grotto

Food: Southern Italian

210 Atwells Ave.

(401) 272-9030

Cool Features: Patio dining

Price: $30 and under
per person

Hours: Monday–Thursday
11:30 a.m.–3:30 p.m.,
5 p.m.–10 p.m.,
Friday 11:30 a.m.–2:30 p.m.,
5 p.m.–10:30 p.m.,
Saturday 5 p.m.-10:30 p.m.,
Sunday 12 a.m.–9 p.m.

Café Paragon

Food: American

234 Thayer St.

(401) 331-6200

Cool Features: Great ambiance

Price: $20 and under
per person

Hours: Daily 11 a.m.–12 a.m.

Cassarino's Restaurant

Food: Italian

177 Atwells Ave.

(401) 751-3333

Cool Features: Romantic
atmosphere

Price: $20 and under
per person

Hours: Monday–Thursday
11:30 a.m.–10 p.m.,
Friday–Saturday
11:30 a.m.–11 p.m.

Casserta's Pizzeria

Food: Pizza, Italian

121 Spruce St.

(401) 272- 3618

Cool Features: Delivery

Price: $20 and under
per person

Hours: Sunday, Tuesday–
Thursday 9:30 a.m.–
10:30 p.m., Friday–Saturday
9:30 a.m.–11:30 p.m.

The Cheesecake Factory

Food: Eclectic and
international

94 Providence Place

(401) 270-4010

Cool Features: Take-out pickup
and online menu

Price: $30 and under
per person

Hours: Monday–Thursday
11:30 a.m.–11 p.m.,
Friday– Saturday
11:30 a.m.–12:30 a.m.,
Sunday 10 a.m.–10 p.m.

Fire + Ice

Food: Asian

48 Providence Place

(401) 270-4040

Cool Features: All-you-can-eat,
personalized stir-fry buffet

Price: $30 and under
per person

Hours: Monday–Thursday
11:30 a.m.–11 p.m., Friday–
Saturday 11:30–12 a.m.,
Sunday 10 a.m.–11 p.m.

The Gatehouse Restaurant

Food: American

4 Richmond Sq.,
Suite 100B

(401) 845-9494

Cool Features: Elegant
athmosphere

Price: $40 and under
per person

Hours: Tuesday–Thursday
5:30 p.m.–10:30 p.m., Friday–
Saturday 5 p.m.–11 p.m.,
Sunday 11 a.m.–3 p.m.,
5 p.m.–9 p.m.

Golden Crust Pizza

Food: Pizza

228 Oakland Ave.

(401) 273-2288

Cool Features: Proximity to
late-night parties

Price: $10 and under
per person

Hours: Monday–Thursday
3 p.m.–2 a.m., Friday–Saturday
11 a.m.–2 a.m., Sunday
12 p.m.–2 a.m.

Hemenway's Seafood Grille and Oyster Bar

Food: Seafood

121 South Main St.

(401) 351-8570

Cool Features: Raw bar

Price: $40 and under
per person

Hours: Monday–Thursday
11:30 a.m.–10 p.m.,
Friday–Saturday 11:30 a.m.–
11 p.m. Sunday 12 p.m.–9 p.m.

Joe's American Bar and Grille

Food: American

148 Providence Pl.

(401) 270-4737

Cool Features: The
revolving door

Price: $20 and under
per person

Hours: Monday–Saturday
11 a.m.–12:30 a.m.

La Creperie

Food: Crepes and salads

82 Foves Aly

(401) 751-5536

Cool Features: Small café
tables

Price: $5 and under per person

Hours: Monday–Thursday
10 a.m.–12 a.m.,
Friday–Saturday 9 a.m.–2 a.m.,
Sunday 9 a.m.–12 p.m.

Lili Wok

Food: Chinese

600 Douglas Ave.

(401) 331-8188

Cool Features: Delivery

Price: $10 and under
per person

Hours: Daily 11:30 a.m.–
11 p.m.

Mai Tai

Food: Asian

101 Mineral Springs

(401) 354-6868

Cool Features: Resealable plastic containers—great for leftovers

Price: $15 and under per person

Hours: Monday–Sunday 11 a.m.–11 p.m.

Meditteraneo

Food: Italian

134 Atwells Ave.

(401) 331-7760

Cool Features: Turns into a Salsa Club on the weekends

Price: $40 and under per person

Hours: Monday–Thursday 11:30 a.m.–9 p.m., Friday 11:30 a.m.–10 p.m. Saturday 11:30 a.m.–11 p.m. Sunday 3 p.m.–9 p.m.

Sicilia's Pizza

181 Atwells Ave.

(401) 273-9222

Cool Features: Delivery

Price: $6 and under per person

Hours: Daily 10:30 a.m.–2 a.m.

Union Station Brewery

Food: American

36 Exchange Terrace

(401) 274-2739

Cool Features: Late-night food

Price: $20 and under per person

Hours: Monday–Thursday 11 a.m.–12:30 p.m., Friday–Saturday 11 a.m.–1:30 a.m.

Uno's Pizzeria

Food: American

82 Providence Place

(401) 270-4866

Cool Features: Athmosphere

Price: $16 and under per person

Hours: Monday–Thursday 11 a.m.–11 p.m., Friday–Saturday 11 a.m.–12 a.m.

Student Favorites:

The Cheesecake Factory
Golden Crust
Lili Wok
Sicilia's Pizza
Uno's Pizzeria

24-Hour Eating?

None

Other Places to Check Out:

Brickway (Breakfast)
Kartabar Restaurant (Mediterranean)
Olives
Phillepe's (Deli)

Best Pizza:

Antonio's Pizza

Best Chinese:

Lili Wok

Best Breakfast:

Admiral Spa Inc.

Best Wings:

Joe's American Bar and Grille

Best Healthy:

La Creperie

Best Place to Take Your Parents:

Blue Grotto
Hemenway's Seafood Grille and Oyster Bar

Closest Grocery Stores:

North Providence Food Mart
1370 Mineral Spring Ave.
North Providence
(401) 353-6760

Shaw's Supermarkets
15 Smithfield Road
North Providence
(401) 353-2075

Whole Foods Market
601 N. Main St.
Providence
(401) 621-5990

Did You Know?

When ordering from Golden Crust, make sure to get bleu cheese and throw in a side of golden fries.

Want more than just a regular slice? **Antonio's specializes in gourmet pizza**. Chicken pesto and tomato basil are to die for!

Meditteraneo's turns into a salsa club after hours on the weekend.

Students Speak Out On...
Off-Campus Dining

"Federal Hill is less than 10 minutes away, and the food there is great. If you're looking for something a little less pricey, the mall has great places like Cheesecake Factory, Fire + Ice, and Uno's. Admiral Spa serves breakfast, as well."

Q "Federal Hill is known for its Italian but can be a little pricey. **Thayer Street also has good restaurants**, but fun shops too! Of course, there is Golden Crust, which you can't miss. It's the local college pizza place."

Q "**Golden Crust** becomes just as much a part of the Providence College student meal plan as Raymond Dining Hall is."

Q "If there is one thing that's great about the city of Providence, it's the restaurants. **There is so much** to choose from. There's great Indian food and great Italian food. There are just so many little places to go and enjoy. Every street has its own gem. There really is something for everyone."

Q "The **Federal Hill area is amazing**—tons of fine Italian food. Blue Grotto and Mediterraneo are delicious; Cassarino's is more popular if you don't want to empty your bank account."

Q "The **restaurants off campus are amazing**. On Thayer Street, I would hit up Kartabar (really interesting Mediterranean food), Phillipe's (for really good wraps and sandwiches), or even Café Paragon (for a slightly nicer sit-down meal.)"

Q "Restaurants are excellent! **Brickway on Wickeden is wonderful for breakfast**. There is Olives if you want a good martini and great jazz music."

Q "**Two words: Fire + Ice**. Usually, when you're going out to eat from school, you're going with a group of friends. Not only is Fire + Ice great food, but it's the easiest to split the bill. It's a buffet and runs about 15 dollars for dinner and even less for lunch. You personalize your own stir fry plate and most importantly, it's all you can eat!"

The College Prowler Take On...
Off-Campus Dining

Providence leaves residents and visitors with a plethora of dining choices. From upscale Italian on Federal Hill to the more eclectic flavors of Thayer Street, the city has something to offer every gourmet, except, of course, the indecisive. Certain local spots become staples in the PC collegiate dining experience. Lili Wok is ideal for ordering in on those frigid nights when it's just too cold to warrant walking anywhere else. When you have stayed out so late, it becomes folly to return home without some sort of nourishment. Many PC students turn to Admiral Spa for sustenance in those wee morning hours. But, at 2 a.m., nothing is more appetizing than a slice of Golden Crust with bleu cheese. (Warning: do not eat sober!) The ritual parents' weekend would not be complete without an outing to Federal Hill, especially when you know the 'rents are paying. While everyone maintains a personal favorite suitable to their palette, all appreciate the innumerable choices available.

The closest thing to a NY slice of pizza is Antonio's on Thayer Street, but unfortunately, they do not deliver. Many eateries do deliver, including Sicilia's on Federal Hill. A drawback to delivery is that in the snow it can take up to two hours. However, some places, such as Mai Tai, accept credit cards for those running short on cash. Dining out and delivery are an excellent option when you've run out of Slavin money and Ray disappoints yet again. Offering a diverse selection of cuisine for all budgets, Providence restaurants subscribe to the old adage: variety is the spice of life.

A-

The College Prowler® Grade on

Off-Campus Dining: A-

A high Off-Campus Dining grade implies that off-campus restaurants are affordable, accessible, and worth visiting. Other factors include the variety of cuisine and the availability of alternative options (vegetarian, vegan, Kosher, etc.).

Campus Housing

The Lowdown On...
Campus Housing

Room Types:

Standard – A regular dorm room from singles to quads with a communal bathroom.

Apartment – Two bedrooms, a common living area, full kitchen, and one bathroom per apartment.

Suite – Two bedrooms, a common living area, half kitchen, one bathroom for a four-person, two bathrooms for a six-person.

Best Dorms:

Aquinas

McVinney

Worst Dorms:

Dore

Guzman

St. Joseph's

Undergrads Living on Campus:

75%

University-Owned Apartments:

5

Dormitories:

Aquinas Hall

Floors: 4

Bathrooms: Community
(1 per floor)

Coed: Yes

Residents: All classes

Room Types: Triples, limited doubles and singles

Special Features: Sinks in the room, 24-hour study lounge, one laundry room per floor, chapel.

Cunningham Hall

Floors: 5

Bathrooms: Private

Coed: Yes

Residents: Upperclassmen

Room Types: 6-person apartments

Special Features: Each apartment contains two bathrooms, a vanity area, kitchen, dining room, living room, and nice bedrooms.

Davis Hall

Floors: 6

Bathrooms: In room

Coed: Yes

Residents: Upperclassmen

Room Types: 4-person apartments

Special Features: Each apartment contains a bathroom, a vanity area, a kitchen, dining room, and two-person bedrooms.

DiTraglia Hall

Floors: 5

Bathrooms: Private

Coed: Yes

Residents: Upperclassmen

Room Types: 6-person apartments

Special Features: Each apartment contains two bathrooms, a vanity area, a living room, dining room, kitchen, and two-person bedrooms.

Dore Hall

Floors: 3

Bathrooms: Community
(1 per half floor)

Coed: Yes

Residents: All classes

Room Types: Singles, doubles, triples, quads

Special features: Laundry room, study lounge, kitchen.

Fennell Hall

Floors: 4

Bathrooms: Community
(2 per floor)

Coed: No (all male)

Residents: Underclassmen

Room Types: Singles, doubles, a few triples and some quads

Special Features: Sinks in the room, large recreation lounge, laundry room, located on the new quad.

Guzman Hall

Floors: 3

Bathrooms: Community (1 per floor)

Coed: No (all male)

Residents: Mostly underclassmen

Room Types: Triples, quads

Special Features: Study and recreational lounge, laundry room, chapel.

Mal Brown Hall

Floors: 5

Bathrooms: Private

Coed: Yes

Residents: Upperclassmen

Room Types: 6-person apartments

Special Features: Each apartment contains two bathrooms, a vanity area, living room, dining room, kitchen, and two-person bedrooms.

McDermott Hall

Floors: 4

Bathrooms: Community (1 per floor)

Coed: Yes

Residents: All classes

Room Types: Triples, quads

Special Features: Study lounge, laundry room, small kitchen, located on quad.

McVinney Hall

Floors: 9

Bathrooms: Community (1 per floor)

Coed: No (all female)

Residents: Freshmen

Room Types: Doubles

Special Features: Kitchen, social lounge, study lounge, laundry room, upper floors have a spectacular view.

Meagher Hall

Floors: 3

Bathrooms: Community (1 per floor)

Coed: No (all female)

Residents: All classes

Room Types: Triples, quads

Special Features: Laundry room, study lounge, located on quad.

Raymond Hall

Floors: 3

Bathrooms: Community (2 per floor)

Coed: No (all female)

Residents: Underclassmen

Room Types: Triples, quads, limited doubles

Special Features: Study lounge, laundry room, dining hall on first floor, kitchen.

St. Joseph's Hall

Floors: 4

Bathrooms: Community
(1 per floor)

Coed: No (all male)

Residents: Underclassmen

Room Types: Triples and quads

Special Features: Study
lounge, recreational lounge,
kitchen, Office of Residence
Life and the Department of
Theology are located in the
basement.

Housing Offered:

Singles: 16%

Doubles: 12%

Triples/Suites: 46%

Apartments: 18%

Other: 8%

Bed Type

Twin extra-long (39"x 80"), bunkable beds, lofting available in
certain dorms

Available for Rent

MicroFridge with microwave

Cleaning Service?

In communal areas including community bathrooms. UNICO
staff comes daily. Apartment bathrooms are not cleaned.

What You Get

Bed, desk, chair, dresser, closet or wardrobe, window shade,
cable TV jack, Ethernet or broadband Internet connection, free
campus and local phone calls

Also Available

Special-interest housing

Did You Know?

Providence College has **banned smoking** in all of the dorms on campus. So smokers should be ready to stand outside.

Students Speak Out On...
Campus Housing

"The dorms are a decent size; compared to other colleges I've seen, they are about average. If you are a freshman male and like to party and be loud, you want to live in Guzman Hall; its opposite would be Fennell Hall."

Q "For girls, **the rooms in Raymond Hall are huge** with tons of closet space. We could have fit a hot tub in the middle of our floor when my roommates and I lived there freshman year. The on-campus apartments are really nice, with all the amenities you can imagine. Living there was like living in a hotel for a year."

Q "The dorms aren't beautiful or anything incredible, but they are fun. **Living on the quad was the time of my life**. Freshman year, I recommend the normal frosh dorms just because you meet all the other freshmen."

Q "All the **dorms are nice in their own way**, but if you want to stay away from the traditional rowdy dorms or the fines that go along with them, I would stay away from McDermott, Guzman, and St. Joe's."

Q "A couple of the dorms are **extremely old fashioned and basically falling apart**, more specifically Fennell and Dore. But these dorms are for those who like the quiet laid-back environment but who are willing to go to upper campus to have fun."

Q "The **dorms are adequate at PC**. They are definitely big enough, and there are plenty of options as to whether you want to live in a double, triple, or quad."

Q "The dorm rooms are pretty big—especially now that they opened the new suites. It creates fewer beds in the rooms and makes it pretty spacious. I think the quad is still a must for sophomores—**a year in the quad is a year well spent**."

Q "The dorms are pretty standard. **The nicest dorm is Aquinas Hall**. This hall is great because all of the rooms have sinks in them, which is a major convenience."

Q "For incoming freshmen I definitely would suggest being in an all freshman dorm. **For girls, McVinney or Raymond**; boys Guzman or probably Guzman, unless you're more quiet and don't mind the walk from lower campus."

Q "It's nothing like home, but it's far from unlivable. I cannot say where to go and where to avoid. **I loved Aquinas and hated Meagher**, but that had nothing to do with the actual building."

The College Prowler Take On...
Campus Housing

Adequate is the best word to describe campus housing. Ranging from old and in need of repairs, to newer suites, campus housing covers the entire gamut of possibilities. Everyone recommends freshmen choosing an all-freshman dorm to create solidarity with their class. Sophomore year on the quad is practically a necessity. Dore and Fennell prove to be for the quiet and laid-back types who prefer single living and longer walks to class. St. Joe's, Guzman, and McDermott can all get a bit rowdy and rack up quite a few fines. Aquinas boasts of having in-room sinks, a short walk to class, and a central location. The all girl dorms—Raymond, Meagher, and McVinney—tend to be quieter and less prone to damages.

Although PC doesn't guarantee housing all four years, it has never had a problem accommodating students in the past. With the addition of the fabulous new suites housing is better than ever. The "new quad" created on lower campus is going to be the place to be. Housing is assigned by Residence Life freshman year based on preference to buildings and room size. A survey provides the basis of roommate assignments, and compatibility generally upholds. After freshman year, a lottery system determines housing, which is annoying if you get a poor time. While space in most of the dorms is sufficient, frustration over crowded laundry rooms is common. Each dorm is equipped with a study lounge, but Aquinas' is the most frequented. Physical plant often needs some serious nudging before taking care of problems, but the new maintenance request line has definitely increased efficiency. Overall, the dorms at PC are not too big, not too small, but just right.

B+

The College Prowler® Grade on
Campus Housing: B+

A high Campus Housing grade indicates that dorms are clean, well-maintained, and spacious. Other determining factors include variety of dorms, proximity to classes, and social atmosphere.

Off-Campus Housing

The Lowdown On...
Off-Campus Housing

Undergrads in Off-Campus Housing:
25%

Average Rent For:
Pinehurst: $850–$1,150/month

Oakland: $950–$1,250/month

Pembroke: $950–$1,250/month

Popular Areas:
Pinehurst, Oakland, Pembroke

For Assistance Contact:
Office of Off-Campus Living

*www.providence.edu/
Student+Life/Living+at+PC/
Off-Campus+Living*

(401) 865-2420

rkless@providence.edu

Best Time to Look for a Place:
Beginning of 1st semester junior year

Students Speak Out On...
Off-Campus Housing

> **"Most students don't live off campus until junior or senior year, but the school is very supportive and helps students find places to live."**

Q "I like living off campus more than on campus because **there's much more freedom**; but, I have to deal with bills and a landlord. Most houses are within a quarter mile from campus, so it's convenient to live off campus, even if you don't have a car."

Q "Housing off-campus is easy to get, and sometimes you can get a deal, but **you have to watch out for the landlords**. Make sure the house you rent is registered with the Office of Off-Campus Living."

Q "I believe **it's worth it if you want to throw parties** and get a sense of life after college, but you tend to miss out on the real college experience when you venture off campus."

Q "I think living off campus is great, and I highly encourage students to do so. There is a policy for students where **they have to obtain permission to move off** before they actually can—I think that is absurd."

Q "I personally don't think it's worth it, given the people I have talked to. **Many of the houses are old** and not in the best locations."

Q "**You need to be a junior or senior to live off campus**, but it is definitely worth it. I lived right off campus (a three-minute walk) both years, and I loved it!"

Q "**Money-wise, it's a little cheaper**, and, hey, you can do whatever you want, but with that comes a lot of other responsibilities."

Q "**Most students stay on junior year and move off senior year**, unless they sign a two-year lease junior year. If you're active on campus, it might make more sense for you to stay on campus so you're not constantly going back and forth."

The College Prowler Take On...
Off-Campus Housing

If you're looking for a smoother transition to post-college life, off-campus housing may be the choice for you. And while all the houses are on the streets immediately surrounding campus, migrating on to campus in the bitter cold may take a little more motivation. Renting an off-campus house may seem like a rule-free college experience, but it comes equipped with its own set of worries, including bills, landlords, and housemates. Some of the houses are poorly maintained, while others are newly renovated. Pinehurst, Oakland, and Pembroke are some popular off-campus streets and usually play host to late-night and ticket parties.

The college now requires students to get permission before they can move off campus, and freshmen and sophomores are required to live on campus. If you decide to move off campus, the Office of Off-Campus Living makes finding a livable space much easier by providing listings of available spaces, cooperative landlords, and people searching for housemates. Living off campus isn't for everyone, but those responsible enough to handle the bills and walking to campus seem to thoroughly enjoy the experience.

The College Prowler® Grade on
Off-Campus Housing: B+

A high grade in Off-Campus Housing indicates that apartments are of high quality, close to campus, affordable, and easy to secure.

Diversity

The Lowdown On...
Diversity

Native American:
Less than 1%

White:
93%

Asian American:
2%

International:
1%

African American:
2%

Out-of-State:
81%

Hispanic:
2%

Political Activity

Providence College is home to both democrats and republicans, liberals and conservatives. The campus lacks political protests, although some members of the student body are extremely active in politics.

Gay Pride

PC is very accepting of its gay community and even has clubs such as SHEPARD to increase awareness, tolerance, and acceptance of gays. RAs usually participate in a SafeZone program as well.

Most Popular Religions

Catholicism. Pastoral Services and the Chaplain's Office direct numerous programs on and off campus for multiple faiths.

Economic Status

PC students are typically from middle or upper-class economic backgrounds.

Minority Clubs

Although PC isn't very diverse, there is a club for just about every ethnicity on campus. The African American Club and Gaelic Society are two noticeably active clubs on campus that sponsor events under the BMSA banner.

Students Speak Out On...
Diversity

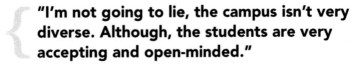

"I'm not going to lie, the campus isn't very diverse. Although, the students are very accepting and open-minded."

Q "Diversity is something PC acknowledges needs work. **Most of the students are Catholic**, and we're not very geographically diverse, either."

Q "**Diversity is definitely lacking at PC**, but everyone gets along, even with those who aren't your 'typical' PC student."

Q "As a student of color, I came into Providence knowing that diversity might be a problem, but as a student, it seems **so unbelievably lacking** that it seems as if it is deliberate."

Q "As far as diversity is concerned, Providence College is lacking. There are **very few minorities on campus**."

Q "We do have the **Balfour Center for Multicultural Students** and the Board of Multicultural Student Affairs, which promote the celebration of diversity on campus, but aside from this our, student body is not very diverse."

Q "You have your **stereotypical PC kid**, and that is what you find everywhere."

Q "**PC has little diversity**. If that is what you are looking for, this is definitely not going to satisfy you."

Q "Economically, most students are middle- and upper-class, and there is a small legion of blatant rich kids. **The faculty is even less diverse than the student body**."

Q "**The only 'minorities' we have in abundance are women**, who seem to be sweeping colleges across the country by storm these days."

Q "The campus is not diverse at all. **White, Catholic and rich pretty much sums up the student body**."

Q "A majority of the kids are either **Italian or Irish**."

The College Prowler Take On...
Diversity

American Eagle or Abercrombie & Fitch? This fairly simple question examines the extent of diversity at PC. The majority of the student body is Caucasian and Christian. The lack of diversity at PC is noted by everyone. While some think it creates a comfortable surrounding, many long for a more diverse campus. There are numerous ethnic clubs on campus such as African American Club, Asian Club, Gaelic Society, and Amigos Unidos that highlight the diversity PC has.

Concern vocalized by the student body has spurned the administration to address the issue. The admissions office cites a 25 percent increase in African American, Asian, and Native American (AHANA) students in the applicant pool for the Class of 2009. There was also an increase in the number of AHANA students invited to enroll at PC. Even with these efforts, diversity remains poor at Providence College. The Balfour Center for Multicultural Affairs helps increase diversity awareness on campus by sponsoring activities and promoting all cultures.

The College Prowler® Grade on
Diversity: D

A high grade in Diversity indicates that ethnic minorities and international students have a notable presence on campus and that students of different economic backgrounds, religious beliefs, and sexual preferences are well-represented.

Guys & Girls

The Lowdown On...
Guys & Girls

Men Undergrads:
42%

Women Undergrads:
58%

Birth Control Available?

No, birth control is not available for sale at the Health Center.

Social Scene

PC is a hugely social school. With all the outgoing people, it is nearly impossible to walk to class without having a conversation with someone. Many students choose to get involved in at least one of the clubs, sports, or organizations at PC. Intermingling and networking are practically core requirements here at Providence College.

Hookups or Relationships?

Many PC students choose commitment-free hookups on the weekends. Although there are couples at PC, their numbers are diminishing, and dating is suffering a slow, painful death. Many people date outside PC.

Did You Know?

Top Places to Find Hotties:

1. PrimeTime
2. Club E's
3. The quad on a sunny day

Top Places to Hook Up:

1. PrimeTime
2. Club E's
3. Dorm rooms
4. Off-campus parties
5. Bradley Café

Best Place to Meet Guys/Girls

The best place to meet guys and girls if you are looking to hook up is probably at the off-campus bars and clubs. Late-night or ticket parties are also a great option. PC is so outgoing that you can meet people just about anywhere from class, to Raymond Dining Hall, or out on the quad.

Dress Code

PC is definitely a preppy school. Polo shirts, button downs, khakis, the whole nine yards. Abercrombie & Fitch, American Eagle, J. Crew all epitomize the PC look. While sweats are okay for early classes, PC students are definitely concerned with what they wear. Jeans and T-shirts are the basic staples. Be prepared to see flip-flops for the greater percentage of the year.

Students Speak Out On...
Guys & Girls

{ **"It's just like anywhere else—you find your groups of people that you fit in with. And of course, we're all hot!"**

Q "I like to think we're a **pretty attractive campus**, at least that's what I've found in the past! You could classify the campus as pretty preppy, but everyone has his or her own twist of style."

Q "There is **something funny about PC students**. Everyone is good looking and has a great smile, and it's without effort. It's an all-American kind of look. The girls are really great, down to earth, and really kind. I have found my best girlfriends at PC. The guys are also great. They won't be the guys at the bar hitting on you, but the ones sticking up for you when that other guy visiting from elsewhere does. You'll notice everyone is always saying hello or waving to 10 people as they walk to and from classes. Overall, the students at PC are good looking, incredibly kind, and know how to have a good time."

Q "The **guys and girls at this school are all the same**: dressed in Abercrombie and accessorized with a silver spoon in their mouths. Though the guys and girls are, for the most part, attractive, they get kind of repetitive."

Q "I think **the girls are pretty good looking**. Most of them are pretty cool and approachable, so it's not hard being friends or even more than friends."

Q "The **guys are good looking at our school,** as are the girls. It's tougher being a girl, however, in that there are definitely more girls than guys on campus."

Q "**Preppy is the word**, I think. I'd say we have a pretty attractive campus."

Q "**There is a lack of guys**, basically, but I have to say I would venture to make the statement that it is a very good-looking campus. In total it is a lot of good-looking people."

Q "The guys can be anywhere from really cool, smart, and interesting to dumb, mean, rude, and immature—the same goes for girls. There are a lot of attractive people at PC, but sometimes, that's as far as it will go. There are **a lot of people at PC who are just there to party** and nothing else. There are a lot of cool people there, though; you just have to find them."

Q "On this matter, I would have to compare PC to a typical high school. **There are different cliques** like jocks, nerds, and those in the middle. Girls are definitely hot, one better than the other. To sum it all up, I would call the majority of the people at PC typical New Englanders."

Q "**A majority of PC students are friendly and polite**. People hold doors for you and smile while passing. The students are smart and hard working. In general, PC has a very good-looking student body!"

Q "The personalities vary completely. They may be lacking in racial diversity, but to me it seems like the people vary a lot in personality—which might be more apparent to me being in the Honors Program. **There are people who party hard, people who play hard**, and people that do both. Many guys and girls are attractive, but compared to some other schools, there's not much pressure to be attractive. It's not a school where girls go anorexic and tanarexic, which is a relief."

Q "I found that after I got to school, I started dressing like my roommates. It's nice because you can go to an early morning class in sweatpants and not stand out, or you could dress to the nines for every class everyday. I've heard horror stories about schools where it's completely unacceptable to wear comfortable clothes—I don't think I'd survive some 8:30 classes without sweat pants! But all-in-all, **people are pretty concerned about appearance**, which I don't think is necessarily a bad thing. I say we wear sweats to 8:30s, but they're still stylish sweats!."

The College Prowler Take On...
Guys & Girls

Caucasian and cute is how many here at Providence would define the "typical" PC student. While the campus overall subscribes to a preppy style, there are those who choose to wear things other than Abercrombie & Fitch. Sweats are not at all unusual for 8:30 classes. There is a significant dearth of males at PC, but the ones that do reside there are good looking for the most part. Females of the attractive variety are available in abundance. Overall, everyone agrees that PC is a good-looking school, even if the look is slightly repetitive.

While PC may look like a page out of a J.Crew ad, one has to wonder if this conformity goes along with the lack of diversity at PC. Pressure to look, dress, and act a certain way may be an influencing factor in PC's stunning good looks. Don't worry if you're not fashion conscious, you'll fit in just fine anyway, because in the case of our campus, beauty is accompanied by brains. One disheartening and noticeable trend is the demise of dating. Fewer couples grace the quad, and drunken hookups, commitment-free of course, are in the vanguard.

The College Prowler® Grade on
Guys: B+

A high grade for Guys indicates that the male population on campus is attractive, smart, friendly, and engaging, and that the school has a decent ratio of guys to girls.

The College Prowler® Grade on
Girls: A-

A high grade for Girls not only implies that the women on campus are attractive, smart, friendly, and engaging, but also that there is a fair ratio of girls to guys.

Athletics

The Lowdown On...
Athletics

Athletic Division:
NCAA Division I

Conference:
Big East, Hockey East

School Mascot:
The Friar

**Males Playing
Varsity Sports:**
67 (4%)

**Females Playing
Varsity Sports:**
101 (5%)

→

Men's Varsity Sports:

Basketball
Cross-Country
Ice Hockey
Lacrosse
Soccer
Swimming & Diving
Track & Field

Women's Varsity Sports:

Basketball
Cheerleading
Cross-Country
Field Hockey
Ice Hockey
Soccer
Softball
Swimming & Diving
Tennis
Track & Field
Volleyball

Club Sports:

Crew
Golf
Racquetball
Rugby (Men's and Women's)
Sailing
Volleyball (Men's and Women's)

Non-Competitive Club Sports:

Martial Arts Club
Outdoors Club
Ski and Snowboarding Club

Intramurals:

3-on-3 Basketball
Dodgeball
Field Hockey
Flag Football
Ice Hockey
Soccer
Tennis
Ultimate Frisbee
Volleyball
Whiffleball

Athletic Fields

Hendricken Field

Getting Tickets

Tickets for the men's basketball game are available through the Ticket Office in Peterson. They are also sold in Ray and Slavin during meal times.

Most Popular Sports

Men's basketball and hockey are the most important sports at PC, drawing local fans as well as alumni. All of the IM sports are popular, especially volleyball, softball, basketball, and hockey.

Overlooked Teams

The women's rugby team is phenomenal. Their trips to nationals have definitely expanded their fan base, though.

Best Place to Take a Walk

Slavin Lawn

Gyms/Facilities

Peterson Recreation Center

Peterson is home to the Taylor Natatorium, Begley Arena, Cuddy Racquetball Complex, and Nautilus weight room. The Taylor Natatorium houses a 25-meter indoor pool with an adjacent outdoor patio. Begley Arena contains five multipurpose courts with a 200-meter running track. These courts accommodate basketball, volleyball, tennis, and indoor soccer, among their other uses. Three courts with observation windows and a dance studio comprise the Cuddy Complex. The outdoor tennis courts have recently been relocated closer to Peterson. As part of the 10-year Campus Master Plan, Peterson will get an addition and a full-service fitness center complete with the latest in strength and cardio equipment.

Mullaney Gym

Mullaney Gym is only for varsity athletics and is the home court for the Lady Friar's basketball team.

Students Speak Out On...
Athletics

> "PC is a Division I school so varsity sports are very popular. Basketball, hockey and lacrosse are everyone's favorites, but all games have pretty good turn-outs."

Q "All sports played on campus are **free, with the exception of men's basketball**. The men play downtown at the Dunkin' Donut's Center, and it's $5 for transportation and admission. Even so, men's basketball is the most popular thing to go to here at PC. We're in the Big East—that means that we play the most competitive teams in the country."

Q "**PC men's basketball is the team of Rhode Island**, so even non-students and alumni get really hyped up for the basketball season. Go Friars!"

Q "Because there aren't that many team sports on campus, **intramurals are huge**. There are also a variety of competitive clubs such as rugby, golf, and sailing."

Q "PC is a Division I school so **varsity sports are a big attraction**. Intramurals are probably just as big, though. The intramural department promotes a fun and easy-going competitive sports program that includes everything from basketball to Frisbee and dodgeball."

Q "I'd say there is **more of a competitive nature among the IM sports**—the majority of students participated in varsity sports in high school and want to continue playing in college."

Q "**Varsity basketball and hockey are the two most popular sports** on campus. Whenever there is a basketball game, the campus is usually buzzing, and these events are great Friday and Saturday night activities."

Q "Men's basketball and hockey are huge. Our **women's rugby team is amazing**, but the guys probably have more fans. Competition on the IM level varies by team and by sport. Some are very competitive, but even beginners can play and have a blast."

Q "**Intramurals are out of control, but they're very, very competitive**, and lots of fun! Everyone wants to win, but is definitely having a good time. To wear an IM championship shirt, you have to be someone special, and everyone on the team will be sporting it the day after the big win."

Q "**It's hard to make a team at PC**, but the school spirit is pretty amazing."

Q "Varsity sports are huge, but intramurals are another way to stay in shape. But you **won't be ostracized if you don't play** any type of sport."

Q "**It's usually a big deal** to win your IM championship game; the prize T-shirts are sought after by many."

The College Prowler Take On...
Athletics

The lights go out, and a spotlight illuminates the door. The crowd is hyped, screaming and counting down the seconds until midnight. Three, two, one and with a deafening roar, the basketball season has officially begun. For all PC students, Late-Night Madness (Formerly Midnight Madness) is one event you must attend. Being a Division I school in the Big East, men's basketball is by far the biggest sport at PC. Friar fanatics pack the Dunk or McPhails to watch the games. School spirit extends to hockey and lacrosse, as well, and generally, all the sports have a decent turn-out. Because most students won't compete on a Division I team, intramurals are huge, yet anyone of any degree of athleticism can play and have tons of fun.

Great school spirit and enthusiasm is a must for any PC student. All sporting events, excluding men's basketball and hockey, are free. Also free are the highly coveted IM championship shirts. With a large selection of IM and club sports, a list that is always growing according to the demands of students, there is no reason why the athletically inclined cannot continue their practice. If it's not already offered at PC, you can start it!

The College Prowler® Grade on

Athletics: B+

A high grade in Athletics indicates that students have school spirit, that sports programs are respected, that games are well-attended, and that intramurals are a prominent part of student life.

Nightlife

The Lowdown On...
Nightlife

Club and Bar Prowler: Popular Nightlife Spots!

Club Crawler:

The clubs in Providence close around 1 a.m. The following are the favorite clubs of PC students, where visiting college students, locals, and PC all converge.

Club Eagle's

Admiral St.

(401) 421-1447

Club Eagle's is the middle ground of local hot spots. It allows for both dancing and conversation and ranges from very casual to dressy in attire. It's a popular hot spot to hit up after Louie's on a Friday night. The cover is normally $3, and you must be 21 to get in. But they aren't too strict on IDs.

Club Hell

73 Richmond St., Downtown

(401) 351-1977

www.club-hell.com

Club Hell is not hugely popular with PC, but when things start feeling, repetitive this place will definitely shake things up. Hell themes its nights; Erotica night on Wednesdays and "Communion" parties on Sundays attract interesting goth characters. You must be 21 to get in.

PrimeTime Café

161 Douglas Ave.

(401) 331-6538

www.primetimeprovidence. com

PrimeTime is the hotspot for PC on Saturday nights. With a usual $3 cover, "PT" (as it is affectionately termed) plays great music and is the perfect dance spot. Things tend to get hot in here so there is no such thing as wearing too little clothing. On Wednesdays, PrimeTime has a drink special of mixed drinks for $1. Needless to say, things can get a little messy. You must be 21 to get in, but they aren't that strict with IDs.

Bar Prowler:

The local watering holes are very near and dear to PC students' hearts. Prices are generally the same wherever you go, except when there's a drink special.

The Abbey

686 Admiral St.

(401) 351-4346

Great for karaoke and for food, the Abbey tends to be an upperclassman bar. It is a relaxed and laid-back environment. You must be 21 to enter.

Bar One

1 Throop Aly, Downtown

(401) 621-7112

Located downtown, this is a classier bar which entices seniors. You have to be 21 to enter, and they are stricter than the local spots on IDs.

Bradley Café

571 Admiral St.

(401) 621-2891

Brad's is a hangout bar great for conversing or playing a little Beirut. The mixed drinks tend to be bigger here than other bars and twice as strong. Thursdays are $2 mixed drinks and they can pretty get crowded. You need to be 21 to get in and cover varies, but usually does not exceed $5.

Fish Co. Bar and Grill

515 S. Water St., Downtown

(401) 421-5796

Fish and Co. is another senior hot spot located downtown. Classier than the usual PC spots, ladies get in free on Thursdays. Fridays and Saturdays, cover charge is $5 and you must be 21 to get in.

Louie's Tap

597 Douglas Ave.

Louie's is the epitome of a hole in the wall bar, but PC students love it. It comes complete with swinging saloon doors for the men's bathroom and a trough to urinate in. Louie's is also popular on Friday nights before heading two doors down to Club E's. You're supposed to be 21 to get in, but Louie's can be pretty relaxed about IDs. Cover is $3.

Patrick's Pub

381 Smith St.

(401) 751-1553

Pat's Pub is a nice local hangout that is more of a sophomore and junior bar. Pat's features tables to order food and drinks, a pool table, and occasionally they host live bands. While there's scarcely room for dancing, people will attempt it anyway. There is no cover charge, and you must be 21 to enter.

Other Places to Check Out:

The Complex

RIRA

Trinity Brewhouse

Bars Close At:

12 or 1 a.m.

Primary Areas with Nightlife:

The streets right off campus, Downtown

Useful Resources for Nightlife:

www.digitalcity.com/ providence/bars

www.frommers.com/ destinations/providence

Cheapest Place to Get a Drink:

Louie's Tap

Favorite Drinking Games:

Beer Pong/Beirut

Card Games (A$$hole, Kings)

Flip Cup

Power Hour

Student Favorites:

Louie's Tap

Patrick's Pub

PrimeTime Café

What to Do if You're Not 21

Chad's

172 Dorrence St. #B3, Downtown
(401) 421-7200

Chad's is a karaoke bar downtown. It can be a great time for the new freshmen who want to go out because, like Remy's, it is 18 and over. The place is tiny, but it's a total blast if you're into singing.

Remy's

203 Westminster St., Downtown
(401) 274-9331

Remy's caters to the 18-and-over crowd on Friday and Saturday nights. Incoming freshmen tend to utilize this club in the beginning of the year, prior to accessing a fake ID. Remy's requires a state ID and a college ID to get in. They also have a dress code of a collared shirt, nice pants (not cargo pants or jeans), and shoes (no sneakers allowed) for males. Although it is 21 to drink, once you're in, it isn't that difficult.

Organization Parties

Many clubs on campus will host parties, be they on or off campus. The African American Club hosts glow parties in '64 Hall, while the lacrosse team may host an off-campus ticket party. Some parties involve alcohol, while others don't, but either way, they are usually a great time.

Frats

See the Greek section!

Students Speak Out On...
Nightlife

"PC is not a dry campus—in fact we have McPhails right on campus where alcohol is served (with proper ID) on the weekends. People don't really party on campus unless they are over 21. Apartment residents will tend to have parties."

Q "Of course, not everyone parties, but there are a lot of us who do. **There are many bars in the area**, and there are fairly frequent theme parties at the off-campus houses."

Q "Maybe I am biased, but **PC knows how to rage**. We throw incredible parties. For instance, the last day of classes, Ridiculousfest has been held for the past few years on Pembroke. The golf party in the beginning of the year is definitely memorable, along with the numerous theme parties that occur. PC students have no problem finding an excuse to celebrate."

Q "I find that **McPhails is one of PC's greatest features**. As for the local bars, if you're looking for a good time, try RIRA or Trinity Brewery. As for the bars around campus, anything can get you in—from good looks to a Blockbuster card."

Q "I am not a huge drinker, and every party on campus or surrounding campus just **involves people hanging around drinking, talking, and playing beer pong** or whatever. I like music and dancing, so as president of a club, I like to get a DJ and try to have parties on campus. Usually, these events do alright, but many people don't come because there is no alcohol involved."

Q "The **different bars take on different personalities**, so there is a fit for everyone."

Q "**Some of the popular places are Brad's and PrimeTime**. On a Friday and Saturday night, these places are packed with all the kids that go to Providence College. It lets you meet people who go to the school and just have a good time."

Q "I think most frosh go downtown at the beginning of the year since you don't need a fake ID to get in. There are places like **the Complex and Remy's for dancing who don't serve minors**, karaoke bars like Chad's, and sports bars like Bar One downtown."

Q "The **bars and clubs are a very good time** and are usually occupied by only PC kids, which is nice in most cases. They are easy to get into and usually pretty safe."

Q "The **party scene at Providence College is crazy**. On campus can be fun, but off campus is where the social scene really takes place at our school."

The College Prowler Take On...
Nightlife

Nightlife at PC consists mainly of drinking at any of the nearby off-campus bars. For a laid-back social night, Brad's or Louie's is the place to be. If getting your groove on is more your speed, PrimeTime Café or Club Eagle's is where it's at. Karaoke at Pat's Pub or the Abbey is always a fun time. Although these are the most frequented bars around campus, freshmen early in the year trek downtown to Remy's or Chad's for an 18-and-over experience. Seniors 21 and over will migrate downtown as well for a classier bar experience at Trinity Brewery or Fish Co. If you don't like to drink, there is always some event occurring on campus sponsored by the Board of Programmers or the SAIL office.

Prices at the bars aren't as steep as in other cities like Boston or New York. Mixed drinks run about $4.50, shots up to $3, and beers for $3 and under. Even so, most students choose to pre-game before the bars to save on spending. There are enough bars that you can always change things up if the usual routine starts feeling repetitive. PC is a party school whether you choose to drink or not, so be prepared for some late nights and rough mornings.

The College Prowler® Grade on
Nightlife: A-

A high grade in Nightlife indicates that there are many bars and clubs in the area that are easily accessible and affordable. Other determining factors include the number of options for the under-21 crowd and the prevalence of house parties.

Greek Life

The Lowdown On...
Greek Life

Number of Fraternities:
0

Number of Sororities:
0

Undergrad Men in Fraternities:
0%

Undergrad Women in Sororities:
0%

Other Greek Organizations:
None

Students Speak Out On Lack of
Greek Life...

{ **"We don't need them! There's so many different ways to meet people and have fun that Greek life would only make things complicated."**

Q "At first, I was a little hesitant about not having Greek life, but I love not having it at PC. Everyone is accepting of everyone else, and there aren't such drastic lines dividing students. **We still have amazing parties**, and there's lots to do and get involved with."

Q "There is **no Greek life at PC**. I find this to be a perk. But, if you're looking for a Greek system as a means for a social life, PC is not a school for you. However, we have clubs on campus that do more for the school and community than a frat or sorority would."

Q "Being a private, Catholic institution, Providence College doesn't feel the need to have Greek life on campus. The only fraternities on campus are academic societies. One thing that is great about going to school in Providence is that **you have the ability to pledge at other schools** in the area, which is an option often taken by PC students."

Q "While there is **no Greek life**, a lot of the different clubs and organizations on campus take on a Greek social life, having houses and 'welcoming parties'; it's a good time."

Q "There are no fraternities or sororities on campus. I honestly think this is one of the best things about the school. **There is no rushing**, and campus is usually pretty quiet compared to those with a Greek system."

Q "Sorry; it's nonexistent. But, in my opinion, it's a good thing; **no one is trying to be anything they are not** to get into a house."

Q "There is no Greek life on campus, but that doesn't mean that there is no fun at PC. **Social life at PC is indescribable**; if one wants to participate in it, that is."

Q "It's **so nice to not have Greek life** at all."

The College Prowler Take On...
Greek Life

There is no Greek scene at PC due to the Roman Catholic affiliation of the college. Because of this, PC students mingle freely without respect to class years or any other restricting criteria.

Many students like the absence of Greek life. Unofficially, a Greek scene comparison can be drawn to several clubs on campus whose extensive interview process may feel like rushing. Following tradition, those who make the club are "initiated" with a night of silly, usually messy, fun.

The College Prowler® Grade on
Greek Life: N/A

A high grade in Greek Life indicates that sororities and fraternities are not only present, but also active on campus. Other determining factors include the variety of houses available and the respect the Greek community receives from the rest of the campus.

Drug Scene

The Lowdown On...
Drug Scene

Most Prevalent Drugs on Campus:

Alcohol
Marijuana

Liquor-Related Referrals:

181

Liquor-Related Arrests:

0

Drug-Related Referrals:

27

Drug-Related Arrests:

0

→

Drug Counseling Programs

Chaplain's Office

(401) 865-2216

Services: Religious pastoral counseling and pastoral care

The Health Educator, Katie Gates

(401) 865-1817

Services: Workshops and screenings

The Personal Counseling Center

(401) 865-2343

Services: Early identification, assessment, and intervention; substance abuse counseling

Student Health Services

(401) 865-2422

Services: Works in cooperation with the Personal Counseling Center in assessing problems

Students Speak Out On...
Drug Scene

"Truthfully, I don't believe there is a lot of drug use on campus. I'm a very social person and have never come across any drugs besides marijuana."

Q "I feel like the drug scene here is pretty mild. **Alcohol is much more prevalent on campus than any drug**. I suppose pot would be the biggest drug used on campus, but it's never been as widespread as alcohol by any means. I've never been in a situation where anything more 'hardcore' than pot was being used, either. There will always be kids that do it, but it's not as common as booze."

Q "Honestly, I don't know much about it. I know it's not overbearing. It's a college campus, **if you want to find drugs, you will**. But it really is not a huge problem at Providence College."

Q "**Marijuana is usually the biggest drug on campus**. But sometimes I hear of individuals taking ecstasy and mushrooms. The drug scene on campus, from what I see, isn't big, but it is still evident."

Q "**Pot is typical**, but for the most part, kids here just like to booze—frequently."

Q "I have not seen much of it at all; **alcohol is a big thing**, but drugs are really not at PC."

Q "**I know it exists**, but I'm not really part of this scene."

Q "From what I know, **I do not think the drug scene is too bad at PC** compared to other colleges across the country. However, there is heavy drinking all over campus, and it is pretty much accepted as the norm."

Q "**I know a lot of people smoke weed**, and I have heard that the school has an underground cocaine scene, but as for seeing it and being associated with it, I cannot comment,.because I do not know about it."

Q "As far as drugs, **there really isn't too much going on**. Marijuana is probably the most popular drug of choice. However, its use is usually pretty quiet."

The College Prowler Take On...
Drug Scene

By far, the most widely used drug at PC is alcohol. Binge drinking is a normal occurrence, and one which every student cannot help but observe. The real drug scene is much more inconspicuous. While marijuana is the drug of choice, there are whispers about ecstasy, mushrooms, and a small coke scene. Drugs can be acquired at PC like most colleges, but the scene is not so prevalent that it cannot be avoided or even go undetected at all.

The low-key use of drugs makes PC a comfortable atmosphere for the students who don't use, while users should be satisfied. The drug scene could be far worse than it is, but drinking, not drugs, is really what PC is about.

The College Prowler® Grade on

Drug Scene: B+

A high grade in the Drug Scene indicates that drugs are not a noticeable part of campus life; drug use is not visible, and no pressure to use them seems to exist.

Campus Strictness

The Lowdown On...
Campus Strictness

What Are You Most Likely to Get Caught Doing on Campus?

- Breaking parietal rules
- Drinking underage
- Fire code violations
- Opening fire doors
- Parking illegally
- Propping doors
- Setting off fire alarms
- Stealing mugs from Ray
- Streaking at the Civ Scream
- Throwing things from windows

Students Speak Out On...
Campus Strictness

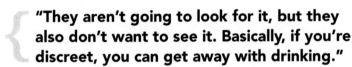

"They aren't going to look for it, but they also don't want to see it. Basically, if you're discreet, you can get away with drinking."

Q "It's your Resident Assistant's job to monitor the alcohol and drug use on campus. It does happen, and more often than not, you'll get along with just a strict warning. But if it becomes a problem, chances are, you will get written up. Then the consequences enforced by the College are steep. **It's a hefty fine and probation**."

Q "**The campus is strict on drugs** and not so strict on drinking. It is a wet campus, and as long as you aren't causing problems, it really is not overly strict on alcohol."

Q "My problem with campus police is that they are not strict at all when it comes to drugs or drinking. **PC is far from being a dry campus**, not because of the many bars surrounding it, but because campus police don't do a good job preventing it."

Q "The **policies are in place**."

Q "The drinking policy and drug policy are pretty strict according to the written rules. As long as its use isn't seen, and people aren't causing a problem, then **it's usually not as strict as the rules suggest**."

Q "**I have yet to run into them**, but I know drinking is not a problem. I would say illegal drugs would be, though."

Q "In my experiences with the campus police and security guards, I have typically found them to be extremely strict as compared with other schools that my friends attend. Security really seems to be ever-present. They are always around, and **they are equipped with magic noses**."

Q "I would say **fairly strict**; I mean, if you are being blatantly obvious about something, they will punish you."

Q "The campus police, as well as the Providence police are **pretty lenient about alcohol**. I'm not too sure about drugs, though."

Q "**Some of the policies are stricter than others**, but drinking cautiously and without disrupting others should not be a problem at PC."

The College Prowler Take On...
Campus Strictness

Policies are in place to punish miscreants, from parking to drug use; however, enforcement of these policies varies. Campus security will hand out parking tickets without hesitation, but they will very rarely conduct searches for suspected drug use. Usually, a warning is given before any penalties are assigned for offenses. If you are written up for an infraction, the fines are steep. A first time alcohol infraction costs $200 and a meeting with your Hall Director. A transport to the hospital for an alcohol related occurrence can be $1,000. The best way to avoid fines and write-ups is to not break the rules, but if you are breaking the rules, avoid being blatant. Most agree that drinking is generally overlooked unless it is disturbing others.

One rule the Providence students detest is parietals. Members of the opposite sex are not allowed in rooms after 12 a.m. during the week and 2 a.m. on the weekends. Although this rule is hardest to enforce in coed dorms, it is strictly enforced in all-female dorms, where the guest log makes it fairly simple to track down vagrant boys. Enforcement of college rules really comes down to the Resident Assistants, although Hall Directors and campus security will occasionally fill out reports, as well. Laid-back RAs are just as common as strict ones, so it's really the luck of the draw. It is better to just be smart about rule-breaking.

B-

The College Prowler® Grade on

Campus Strictness: B-

A high Campus Strictness grade implies an overall lenient atmosphere; police and RAs are fairly tolerant, and the administration's rules are flexible.

Parking

The Lowdown On...
Parking

Approximate Parking Permit Cost:
It's free!

Common Parking Tickets:
No permit: $10 ticket and possible towing
Handicapped zone: $25
Fire lane: $50

Student Parking Lot?
Yes

Freshmen Allowed to Park?
No

→

Parking Permits

Upperclassmen get priority for parking permits. Permits are issued on first-come, first-serve basis. Only in extenuating circumstances, such as a medical concern, will freshman and sophomores be given permits.

Did You Know?

Best Places to Find a Parking Spot
Fennell Lot
Dore Lot
Schneider Lot

Good Luck Getting a Parking Spot Here!
Slavin Lot

Students Speak Out On...
Parking

{ **"You need a parking pass to park without being ticketed, and juniors and seniors are allowed to have cars."**

 "Parking is an issue at PC—there's not a whole lot of it. We're in the **process of building an underground parking garage** that will hopefully alleviate some of the congestion in the existing lots. For now, though, it's pretty bad."

Q "I **find it easy to live on campus and park my car** once I have a sticker. Commuters might have a different opinion on how easy parking is, though."

Q "Honestly, it's **pretty shoddy**."

Q "I typically find that **parking is difficult**. For the number of students, there really isn't very much parking."

Q "**Only juniors and seniors are allowed parking**. The parking that is available is pretty close and convenient."

Q "Well, **if you have a sticker it is easy to park**; if not, you may not find your car where you left it in the morning."

Q "It is tough to find spaces at times. They give more passes out than there are spaces. Wait until you need to have a car (like for internships) before you bring one. **They can be more of a nuisance than necessity**."

Q **"You will usually find a parking space**; it's just a matter of where the parking space is and how far it is from where you live on campus! All in all though, the parking situation isn't terrible. They have become more strict with towing recently."

Q **"Parking sucks**—don't bring a car if you don't absolutely need it because you will not be able to find a spot."

Q "With the constant building of new facilities, on-campus parking is becoming extremely scarce for both students and faculty. **It is extremely hard to get parking passes** and, even with a parking pass, spaces are limited."

The College Prowler Take On...
Parking

Parking is a serious campus concern. Freshmen and sophomores are not allowed to have cars on campus unless there are extenuating circumstances. For those juniors and seniors who do bring a car to campus, spots may be hard to come by or require a short hike to the dorm. Security hands out passes on a first-come, first-serve basis, but specific spots aren't assigned to cars. Parking off campus on the nearby streets can be just as difficult due to no parking zones, specific times for parking, and the local residents. Having a car on campus can end up being more of a hassle than it is worth.

The suites and Fine Arts Center have eliminated the parking field on lower campus. And even though security tickets cars without passes, a plethora of students bring their cars up right before breaks, only exacerbating the dismal situation.

The College Prowler® Grade on

Parking: C-

A high grade in this section indicates that parking is both available and affordable, and that parking enforcement isn't overly severe.

Transportation

The Lowdown On...
Transportation

Ways to Get Around Town:

On Campus

PC shuttle service,
Monday–Thursday, Sunday
6 p.m.–1:30 a.m.
Friday–Saturday 9 p.m.–2 a.m.

PC Escorts 6:30 p.m.–1:30
a.m. in library, Harkins, and
Slavin. Call (401) 865-2391 for
assistance

Public Transportation

Rhode Island Public
Transportation Authority
(RIPTA), (401) 781-9400.
Pick up bus schedules from the
Security Office

Taxi Cabs

East Side Taxi
(401) 521-4200

Metro Taxi
(401) 331-8888

Patriot Taxi
(401) 272-1999

Red and White Cab
(401) 521-4200

→

Car Rentals

Avis
local: (401) 521-7900
national: (800) 831-2847
www.avis.com

Budget
local: (401) 751-5401
national: (800) 527-0700
www.budget.com

Enterprise
local: (401) 946-3888
national: (800) 736-8222
www.enterprise.com

Hertz
local: (401) 354-0052
national: (800) 654-3131
www.hertz.com

Thrifty
local: (401) 831-3000
national: (800) 847-4389
www.thrifty.com

Best Ways to Get Around Town

Bribe a friend with alcohol or gas money

Cabs

RIPTA – Free with your student ID

Your own two feet

Ways to Get Out of Town:

Airlines Serving Providence

Air Canada
(888) 247-2262
www.aircanada.ca

American Airlines
(800) 433-7300
www.americanairlines.com

(Airlines Serving Providence, Continued)

Cape Air
(800) 352-0714
www.flycapeair.com

Delta
(800) 221-1212
www.delta-air.com

Grand Bahamas
(800) 545-1300
www.grand-bahama.com

Independence Air
(800) 359-3594
www.flyi.com

Northwest
(800) 225-2525
www.nwa.com

Southwest
(800) 435-9792
www.southwest.com

United
(800) 241-6522
www.united.com

US Airways
(800) 428-4322
www.usairways.com

SATA International
(800) 762-9995
www.sata.pt

Airport

T.F. Green Airport
(888) 268-7222

T.F. Green Airport is 9 miles and approximately 16 minutes driving time from Providence College.

How to Get to the Airport

Airport Express
(401) 521-4200

RIPTA's Airport Shuttle can be boarded at Kennedy Plaza.
(401) 781-9400

A cab ride to the airport costs $25.

Greyhound

The Greyhound bus terminal is located downtown in Providence's Kennedy Plaza, approximately 3 miles from campus. For schedule information, call
(800) 231-2222.

Providence Greyhound Trailways Bus Terminal
Kennedy Plaza
Providence, RI 02903
www.greyhound.com

Amtrak

The Amtrak train station is in downtown Providence, approximately 2.5 miles from campus. For schedule information,call
(800) 872-7245.

Providence Train Station
100 Gaspee St.
Providence
(401) 727-7379

Travel Agents

Providence Travel Inc.
229 Thayer St.
(401) 521-4545

Suburban Travel Agency
1375 Mineral Springs Ave.
(401) 353-6770

Students Speak Out On...
Transportation

"The Rhode Island Public Transportation Authority has a bus stop right on campus, allowing the students to get around very easily. The bus can also take you to the train station and airport."

Q "**We have a bus stop right on campus**; it takes about 10 minutes to go downtown. Otherwise, we have the PC shuttle that run loops around the immediate community. So, it's really easy to get wherever you need to go."

Q "**Boston is an easy hour bus ride**, and the commuter train will also take you in. Both are cheap."

Q "**Public transportation is the main way to travel** for most PC students."

Q "**Public transportation is semi-convenient**. It depends on where you are trying to go."

Q "**It is extremely easy**; the bus picks us up at the gates, and you could take that to anywhere in RI. On a side note, bring a schedule with you. You never actually make the bus you were planning on, especially the return trip."

Q "**PC does an excellent job with transportation**. You are not allowed to have a car at PC essentially for the first two years you are on campus. However, to make up for that, there is a shuttle driven around the neighborhood on nights and weekends."

Q "It's great! **With our college ID, we can transport ourselves anywhere** on the bus system for free, statewide."

Q "I have found **the greatest form of transportation**—it's called 'take your friend's car.'"

Q "The T is slow, and it's even slower in the winter. **Here is a tip: take the bus**. Even though they aren't always going to get you to your exact destination, the transportation is much more convenient."

Q "Public transportation is super-convenient when it is running. Unfortunately, **the hours of operation are limited**, which means if you go off campus for a party, you may have to split a cab with friends for the way home."

The College Prowler Take On...
Transportation

As per a contract with RIPTA, PC students may ride the buses for free with their student ID throughout the state of Rhode Island. There is a bus stop right outside the campus gates on Huxley Avenue, making RIPTA a convenient mode of transportation. The trolley services are a subsection of RIPTA and therefore also free. Taking a cab is always convenient with the overwhelming number of cab companies to choose from. Cabs are a great option if you want to get somewhere without having to worry about schedules. The college also runs shuttles for the neighborhood loop (convenient for bar-hoppers), and the Metro shuttles people to PrimeTime Café every Saturday night. The train station is just minutes away, as is the bus depot in Kennedy Plaza. Practically every mode of transportation is available, and students unanimously agree on its convenience.

While the RIPTA contract has optimized the shuttle services needed by PC students, the buses often run behind schedule, which can be a hassle. But who can complain when the service is free? During big holidays such as Thanksgiving and Easter, PC provides transportation to the airport for a nominal fee. Generally, it is fairly easy to get around the neighborhood and city of Providence, thanks to convenient and cheap transportation options.

The College Prowler® Grade on

Transportation: B+

A high grade for Transportation indicates that campus buses, public buses, cabs, and rental cars are readily-available and affordable. Other determining factors include proximity to an airport and the necessity of transportation.

Weather

The Lowdown On...
Weather

Average Temperature:		Average Precipitation:	
Fall:	54 °F	Fall:	3.8 in.
Winter:	31 °F	Winter:	3.9 in.
Spring:	48 °F	Spring:	4.0 in.
Summer:	71 °F	Summer:	3.3 in.

Students Speak Out On...
Weather

> "It's New England—we have all the seasons, so bring everything from shorts and skirts to winter jackets."

Q "**Summers are hot**, winters are cold, spring and fall are nice. Peak summer months can get up to the high 80s, and winters can be single digits. It snows, but it rains more often. Bring clothes for every type of weather—T-shirts and shorts, swimsuits, parkas, sweaters, jeans, everything."

Q "Moderate. Winters are cold, and it snows a decent amount. Fall is really nice. It starts to get warm the last few weeks of class and finals in the spring semester. The biggest clothing advice I can give is **bring a gross jacket that you don't care about losing or getting gross** for the long, cold walk to the bars."

Q "In the very beginning of the academic year, it's warm, then it drops to **frigid temps till about the end of April**."

Q "**In the winter, the temperatures are absolutely freezing**, and it is often raining and damp outside. But the warm people on campus make the New England weather a little less harsh."

Q "You never know if its going to be 70, 90, 30, or below freezing. **The weather varies**, and I would say pack something for every kind of weather."

Q "One day it could be blazing hot and the other freezing cold. I live in New Jersey so **I just bring my whole wardrobe at once**."

Q "Welcome to New England—**the weather is very typical of New England, but unpredictable**. It could be 65 one day and snowing the next. You need a little of everything, but definitely some warm clothes for the winter."

Q "New England weather—**be prepared for anything**."

Q "In the past few years, it has rained a lot for some reason, so **an umbrella is always a must have**."

Q "If you live in New England, you could easily adjust to the weather. **Providence is extremely cold in winter and very hot in the summer**. There are really no surprises in the weather."

The College Prowler Take On...
Weather

Be prepared: New England has all four seasons. When you arrive in September, you'll still be wearing summer clothes, sleeping with the windows open, and cranking the fan up to high. Shortly thereafter, a drastic change occurs and suddenly it's fall, and the foliage on campus achieves its peak autumnal beauty. As quickly as fall comes, it leaves, banishing those red and golden leaves to the ground. As they scatter and brown, a notable temperature drop takes place, and soon, flutters of snowflakes float on the crisp winter air. Winters in Rhode Island can be harsh, dropping below zero with the wind chill factor. A rainy season makes up the majority of the spring, although there will be those few gloriously sunny days. Pack for all the seasons and all types of weather.

The one drawback of weather on the PC campus is the constant presence of wind. While maybe only seven days of the school year offer heavy, still air that clings about the body, the majority are characterized by a chilling and bitter wind. "Blustery" best describes the campus weather, so be sure to take a jacket with you. While competing with the wind may sound daunting, Providence can brag of a diversity of experience in regards to weather. The autumn leaves can't be beat, and the downy blankets of snow that occasionally grace the campus charm the aesthetic sense.

The College Prowler® Grade on
Weather: C

A high Weather grade designates that temperatures are mild and rarely reach extremes, that the campus tends to be sunny rather than rainy, and that weather is fairly consistent rather than unpredictable.

Report Card Summary

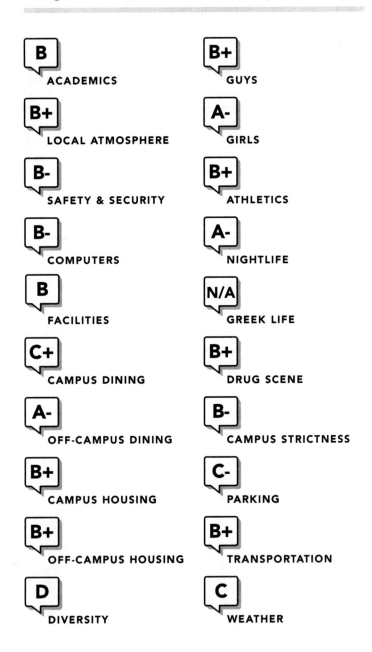

B ACADEMICS

B+ LOCAL ATMOSPHERE

B- SAFETY & SECURITY

B- COMPUTERS

B FACILITIES

C+ CAMPUS DINING

A- OFF-CAMPUS DINING

B+ CAMPUS HOUSING

B+ OFF-CAMPUS HOUSING

D DIVERSITY

B+ GUYS

A- GIRLS

B+ ATHLETICS

A- NIGHTLIFE

N/A GREEK LIFE

B+ DRUG SCENE

B- CAMPUS STRICTNESS

C- PARKING

B+ TRANSPORTATION

C WEATHER

Overall Experience

Students Speak Out On...
Overall Experience

{ **"PC is the perfect school—I wouldn't want to be anywhere else. I love it here. There is something about this school; honestly, I have never found someone who didn't absolutely love it!"**

Q "**I could not imagine myself anywhere but here.** Socially, intellectually, and emotionally, I have grown so much in the past three years. I've met my absolute best friends in the entire world. I've learned about everything from medieval art, to the church in today's world, to Web page making. The best advice that I have to give is to get involved."

Q "I am absolutely and completely in love with Providence College. I transferred after my first semester of freshman year at Virginia Tech. I had the opportunity to experience another kind of school. **PC offers so much in its well-rounded academic** education and its opportunities to meet other amazing students that attend PC. But under no circumstance do I wish I was somewhere else. I am sad to say I only have two years left, and I hope these years go by as slow as possible because the last year and a half have been the best time of my life."

Q "School is pretty good. The academic schedule at PC is very challenging, with teachers who really push their students to the limit, which is important for intellectual growth. Also, **I have made long-lasting relationships with people** on campus, so I really couldn't see myself anywhere else. Although I had the opportunity to go to tons of other schools with better varsity teams, Greek life, campuses, and maybe even better-looking girls, I think I made the right choice with Providence College."

Q "This is the only place I can see myself becoming who I am today. Providence College **provides the means to have people reach their potential**. This school is awesome."

Q "I have absolutely **loved my time on campus**. This is the time in your life to grow and experience life on your own. No other time is like this. I wouldn't trade my experience at Providence College for anything in the world."

Q "I love the strong faith that many of my peers have. I have grown spiritually a lot since I have been here. **My only regret is that I sort of miss home**, but I'm not sure I'd be happier at UVM."

Q "We go to class but we know how to have fun. A teacher once told me, 'Never let class get in the way of an education.' **PC is a hands-on learning experience in all areas**, and I would recommend it to anyone who can balance a social life and school."

Q "I cannot imagine my life had I not come to PC. Between what I have learned, both academically and personally, and the people I have met, **I cannot say enough good things about this school**—just that I am so happy that I chose to come to PC."

Q "I've really enjoyed my time at PC. **There is a good party scene** and a lot of young people who want to have fun. However, it is also a good environment to get a solid, all-around education. There are also a lot of opportunities to get involved in the Providence College community. It all depends on how much you are willing to put into your experience. I feel I have been very active in my three years here, and because of that, I have thoroughly enjoyed my time at PC."

Q "PC has given me everything that another college would have given me. **I don't regret coming to Providence College at all**."

Q "I never once for one second felt that I made a wrong decision choosing Providence. There were hard moments beginning freshman year (everyone has a breakdown now and then, but overall, I made the best friends I always heard that I would make in college. **I want my future kids to go to PC!**"

Q "I love PC! It is the only place I want to be. I know this sounds so cheesy, but it has shaped me to be who I am today. It has done everything for me that a college should do for a student. I have made wonderful, caring friends and **have established myself, and I feel totally comfortable** here. If I could give any advice, it would be to come and take a tour of the school. See the students and meet the students. You will have a chance to see how happy they are, and you will want to come to PC, too!"

Q "I love it. **I wouldn't want to be anywhere else**. I love the people, and I love the family feeling. It's the perfect size and fosters the perfect social life"

The College Prowler Take On...
Overall Experience

Looking back on their time at PC leaves students glowing with fond memories. Most appreciate the stimulating academics and whirlwind social scene that PC offers. While the occasional bout of homesickness is unavoidable, no one remarked that they were unsatisfied with their experience at PC. The worst response is a feeling of mere adequacy, that they received all they would have received at another school. The overwhelming majority look on their time spent at PC as a phenomenal learning experience that has assisted in developing them into the intellectually, emotionally, and socially well-rounded beings that they are today.

The brilliance of the education at PC is that it extends itself outside of the classroom. Your experience of PC can be anything that you want to make it. If you want to focus on academics, you can, and you will find a group of people who feel exactly the same way you do. If you want an education in socializing or just want your college years to be the wild and crazy ones you've heard they can be, PC has that, too. Most students come to PC ready to work and ready to have fun; as long as you are open-minded, PC will give you everything you desire.

The Inside Scoop

The Lowdown On...
The Inside Scoop

PC Slang:

Know the slang, know the school. The following is a list of things you really need to know before coming to PC. The more of these words you know, the better off you'll be.

Angel – Internal Internet site used by teachers to post grades, message boards, and assignments.

Aquinas Chapel – No longer utilized chapel that is becoming a favorite place for study.

BOP – Board of Programmers, organizes most of the on-campus events.

Bursar – Office where you go for new ID cards and for tuition issues.

Cyberfriar – PC's banner Web site used for registration, grades, and other records.

Fishbowl – The all-glass room in Slavin Center.

The Fountain – Located on lower campus, hidden and discreet, there are rumors of "baptisms" occurring here.

→

Friars – Members of a club on campus that give tours, noted for their highly coveted, über-cool white blazers; also, the Dominican Friars who run the school.

HDs – Hall Directors, run dormitories on campus.

Hollywood – The coolest Security Guard on campus.

The Lion's Den – McDermott Residence Hall.

The New Quad – The new quad in front of the Smith Fine Arts Center—is now *the* place to be on campus.

The Quad – Area that should be grassy but isn't; in front of Aquinas Hall.

Ray – Raymond Hall cafeteria.

The Scowl – The yearly April Fool's newspaper put out by the school newspaper *The Cowl*.

Slay – Slavin Center containing Student Center, McPhails, and Alumni Food Court.

The Tunnels – Intricate set of underground tunnels connecting buildings on lower campus.

UA – Urban Action, a volunteer community service organization.

Things I Wish I Knew Before Coming to PC

- Get your housing form in ASAP.
- Do Urban Action your freshman year.
- It's cool to wear a white blazer and give tours.
- Don't buy bedding from the school catalog.
- It's a huge party school.
- Civ sucks.
- Everyone runs for Congress.
- How important the Newport trip really was.
- It's great to be undeclared.
- Anti-virus computer software is a must.

Tips to Succeed at PC

- Schedule classes at times you'll actually go.
- Get all your work done in the afternoon, then nap so you can go out at night.
- Check your e-mail all the time.
- Get AIM+ or Dead AIM (to check drunken IM log).
- Don't be afraid to explore different subjects; you have to fulfill core anyway.
- Ask friends about professors before scheduling classes.
- Always have a back-up for your schedule choices; come registration morning, you'll need it.
- Smile and say hi; don't worry, we'll all wave back.

PC Urban Legends

- The Dore basement is haunted.
- Aquinas 4th floor is haunted by the girls who died in the fire many years ago (no really, it is).
- McDermott Hall is ranked as one of the most promiscuous dorms in the country.

School Spirit

Providence students are full of pep and vigor, particularly when it comes to their school. There are black-out games where fans wore all black, and when it comes to men's basketball, anything goes. The new logo is definitely an improvement, and everyone owns a closet full of PC apparel. PCers are definitely united around our sports teams, although they show this school spirit when discussing the school itself. Although some are not as enthusiastic as others, the majority of students love PC and share that love with anyone and everyone.

Traditions

The Clam Jam

The Clam Jam is an annual event coordinated by BOP. Held on Hendricken field there is food, games, and music. It is key to stop by the Clam Jam even if it is just en route to going out. There are alcoholic beverages for those with proper ID, but many get around that by pre-gaming before they go. It's a great way to start off the year, kick off the weekend, and spend a fun night on campus.

Mr. PC

Mr. PC isn't just like any other beauty pageant. It gives the women of PC, who do outnumber the men, a chance to oogle some of PC's finest specimens. Annually, one male will be crowned Mr. PC after displaying casual style, a talent, formal wear, and answering a question put to them by the judges. Mr. PC was once graciously hosted by Dennis Haskins, better known as *Saved by the Bell*'s Mr. Belding. Mr. PC always promises a few laughs, even if they aren't accompanied by a "Hey-hey-hey, what's going on here?" from television's favorite principal.

Sophomore Outdoor Ball

Sophomore Outdoor Ball, or SOB, is a fantastic night for the sophomore class to come together, get dressed up, and party the night away. Traditionally it is held in a tent on Hendricken field, although preparations are made to move it indoors if it rains. Although stilettos may sink into the soft grass, the night is one of the most memorable events of sophomore year. In true PC style, many of those you encounter at SOB may be under the influence of alcohol, which can make the dance floor slightly dangerous, but fun nonetheless. You may even get a glimpse of PC security shaking their groove thing as the night progresses.

Junior Ring Weekend

Junior Ring Weekend is better known as JRW and is the culmination of a year long preparation by the JRW Core. The entire weekend is themed and focuses around the junior class receiving their class rings. While JRW events begin the end of sophomore year with Ring Premiere, the real fun is the weekend that epitomizes the junior year at PC. Nothing compares to JRW, except maybe the week-long events of graduation. Friday night of this weekend is better known as Club Night, where the junior class and their dates head out to a club rented out specifically for them. The following night is Formal Night, another opportunity to dress to the nines. The class is taken to a secret location, usually a banquet hall or hotel ballroom, where they proceed to relive Club Night, only in formal attire. Sunday's ceremonies include a mass, where the rings are blessed and distributed, and brunch. Everyone looks forward to JRW, stresses over getting a date, and knows what they will wear practically by the end of freshman year.

Newport Trip

The Newport Trip is availble to incoming freshman for a fee of about $25. Labor Day, while all the returning students are cramming on to campus and unloading their stuff, the freshmen are taken by bus to Newport where they are free to spend the day however they choose. Usually, the day's events consist mainly of walking, shopping, eating, and maybe visiting a few mansions, but the Newport trip is the perfect opportunity to get to know your fellow classmates. Besides, who doesn't like spending a day at the beautiful seaport?

Late-Night Madness

Once called Midnight Madness, this event marks the official start to the basketball season, which at PC, is a big deal. The night is spent in the Mullaney gym awaiting the strike of 12 when the basketball teams can officially begin practice sessions. Midnight Madness usually sports a variety of entertainment acts including games, music, free T-shirts, and the Pep Band. The cheerleaders and dance team both do a routine, although the latter is always better than the former. Since PC is so big on sports and school spirit, this is a must-attend event.

Finding a Job or Internship

The Lowdown On...
Finding a Job or Internship

If finding a job after you graduate is a high priority concern, as it is for many PC students, assistance is available through a number of services from the Career Services Center. Taking advantage of PC's friendly social environment is always a great idea as well.

Advice

Career Services can assist anyone who is looking for career guidance. Utilizing their services is just as important freshman and sophomore year as it is junior and senior year. Conference notifications and career opportunities are often sent directly to your mailbox.

Career Center Resources & Services

Career counseling career research
Career workshops and employment fairs
Exploring majors
Graduate school advising
Internships
Interviewing
Networking
On-campus recruitment
Resumes and correspondence
Shadowing program

Grads Who Enter the Job Market Within

6 Months: N/A
1 year: 69%

Firms that Most Frequently Hire Graduates

Fidelity Investments, Deloitte Touche, Merrill Lynch,
PriceWaterhouse Coopers, State Street Bank & Trust

Alumni

The Lowdown On...
Alumni

Web Site:
www.providence.edu/alumni

Office:
Office of Institutional
Advancement
Harkins Hall 107 & 109
Providence, RI 02918
alumni2@providence.edu
(401) 865-2414

Services Available:
Alumni online directory
E-mail

→

Major Alumni Events

The biggest alumni events are reunion weekend and Homecoming weekend. Reunion weekend takes place in June and features numerous events for different class years. Homecoming weekend in February is always a huge success, and alumni usually return to the local watering holes in the evening treating students to free rounds.

Alumni Publications

Providence Digest, The Spectrum, Providence Magazine

Providence Digest comes out quarterly while *Providence Magazine* is printed three times annually. *The Spectrum*, however, is a biweekly periodical. Both students and alumni participate in the writing and operation of this media outlet.

Did You Know?

Robert C. Gallo (Class of '59) – Founder and director of the Institute of Human Virology

Lenny Wilkens (Class of '60) – NBA Hall of Fame player and coach of the NY Knicks

Arthur F. Ryan (Class of '63) – Chairman and CEO of Prudential Insurance Company of America

Lindsay Waters (Class of '69) – Executive Editor for the Humanities and Harvard University Press

Mike Leonard (Class of '70) – NBC News feature correspondent

Elizabeth Flynn Lott (Class of '82) – Executive Vice President of J. P. Morgan Chase and Co.

Doris Burke (Class of '87) – Basketball analyst/reporter, ESPN, ABC Sports, Madison Square Garden Network

Student Organizations

Most of the student organizations listed below can be accessed from the Providence College Web site under Student Life Student Activities.

A Capella Club

African-American Society

Alembic

Anaclastic

Art Club

Art Journal

Amigos Unidos

Asian American Club

Blackfriars Theatre

Board of Multicultural Student Affairs (BMSA)

Board of Students Supporting Athletics

Circolo Italiano

Clube Portugues

College Democrats

College Republicans

Commuter Club

Concert Band

Concert Corale

Cowl

Crew Club

Dance Company

Dance Team

Figure Skating Club

French Club

Friars Cell

Gaelic Society

Golf Club

Intramural Athletic Board (IAB)

Japanese Animation Club

Jazz Band

Liturgical Choir

Off Campus Residence

Orchestra

PC Band

PC Women's Chorus

SHEPARD

Special Guest

Stage Band

Strictly Speaking

Strategic Games Club

Student Environmental Action Coalition

Student Global AIDS Coalition

Students Organized Against Racism (SOAR)

UMADD PC

Veritas

WDOM-FM

Women Will

The Best & Worst

The Ten **BEST** Things About PC

1	Being in a city
2	Restaurants
3	Bars and ticket parties
4	Civ scream
5	Rejects on the rise
6	Movies on Slavin lawn
7	SOB/JRW
8	Blackfriars Theater
9	The renovated library
10	Raymond Hall staff

The Ten **WORST** Things About PC

1. Diversity
2. Parking
3. Ray food
4. Windtunnels
5. Nautilus weight room
6. Civ
7. Parietals
8. Boy/girl ratio
9. Our cheerleaders
10. No grass on the quad

Visiting

The Lowdown On...
Visiting

Hotel Information:

The Biltmore
Kennedy Plaza
Providence, RI 02903
(401) 421-0700
Distance from Campus:
3 miles
Price range: $150 and up

Christopher Dodge House Bed and Breakfast Hotel
11 West Park St
Providence, RI 02908
(401) 351-6111
Distance from Campus:
1.4 miles
Price Range: $129 and up

→

Courtyard Providence

32 Exchange Terrance at
Memorial Blvd.

Providence, RI 02904

(401) 272-1191

Distance from Campus:
2.5 miles

Price Range: $225 and up

Holiday Inn Downtown

195 Atwells Ave.

Providence, RI 02904

(401) 831-3900

Distance from Campus:
1.5 miles

Price Range: $129 and up

Old Court Bed and Breakfast

144 Benefit St.

Providence, RI 02906

(401) 751-2002

Distance from Campus:
2 miles

Price Range: $125 and up

The Providence Marriott

Charles and Orms Streets

Providence, RI 02904

(401) 272-2400

Distance from Campus:
1.5 miles

Price Range: $179 and up

Raddisson Hotel Providence Harbor

220 India Point

Providence, RI 02903

(401) 272-5577

Distance from Campus:
4.5 miles

Price Range: $129 and up

State House Inn

43 Jewett St.

Providence, RI 02908

(401) 351-6111

Distance from Campus:
1.3 miles

Price Range: $139 and up

The Westin

1 West Exchange St.

Providence, RI 02903

(401) 598-8000

Distance from Campus:
2 miles

Price Range: $175 and up

Take a Campus Virtual Tour

www.providence.edu/tour/splash.html

To Schedule a Group Information Session or Interview

Call (800) 721-6444 or (401) 865-2535 for reservations.

Campus Tours

During the summer, campus tours are given Monday through Friday during the summer and Monday through Saturday during the year. Dates and times are available on the monthly visit schedule on the PC Web site. No need to call in advance, tours leave from 222 Harkins Hall.

Day Visits

Day visits to PC are available by reservation at (800) 721-6444. The student will accompany an Admissions Ambassador to two classes, interact with students and faculty, and enjoy lunch in one of the dining halls. Reservations are limited and must be scheduled at least two weeks in advance.

Directions to Campus

Driving from the North

- Follow I-95 South to Rhode Island Exit 23 (Charles Street).
- Proceed right onto Charles Street 0.2 miles to the first light at Admiral Street.
- Take a left onto Admiral Street and proceed approximately 1.2 miles to the third light at River Avenue.
- Take a left onto River Avenue light (0.4) miles at Eaton Street.
- The gate of the campus will be on your left.

Driving from the South

- Take I-95 North to Rhode Island Exit 23.
- Turn right onto Orms Street.
- At light, veer right onto Douglas Avenue (Route 7).
- Proceed 0.7 miles to the third light and make a left onto Eaton Street.
- Proceed about 0.6 miles to the second light at the intersection of Eaton Street and River Avenue. The gate of campus will be on your right.

Driving from the East

- Take I-195 West to I-95 North, to Rhode Island Exit 23 (State Offices).
- Turn right onto Orms Street.
- After the light, veer right onto Douglas Avenue (Route 7).
- Proceed 0.7 miles to the third light and make a left onto Eaton Street.
- Proceed 0.6 miles to the second light at the intersection of Eaton Street and River Avenue. The gate of campus will be on your right.

Driving from the West

- Take I-84 to Route 2 East.

- Follow Route 2 East to Norwich, CT and then take I-395 North along I-395 North to Route 6 East.

- Take Route 6 east into Johnston, RI.

- Proceed along Route 6 to Route 10 North.

- Take I-95 North to Rhode Island Exit 23 (State Offices).

- Turn right onto Orms Street. After the first light, veer right onto Douglas Avenue (Route 7).

- Proceed 0.7 miles to the third light and make a left onto Eaton Street. Proceed 0.6 miles to the third light at the intersection of Eaton Street and River Avenue.

- The gate of the campus will be on your right.

Words to Know

Academic Probation – A suspension imposed on a student if he or she fails to keep up with the school's minimum academic requirements. Those unable to improve their grades after receiving this warning can face dismissal.

Beer Pong/Beirut – A drinking game involving cups of beer arranged in a pyramid shape on each side of a table. The goal is to get a ping pong ball into one of the opponent's cups by throwing the ball or hitting it with a paddle. If the ball lands in a cup, the opponent is required to drink the beer.

Bid – An invitation from a fraternity or sorority to 'pledge' (join) that specific house.

Blue-Light Phone – Brightly-colored phone posts with a blue light bulb on top. These phones exist for security purposes and are located at various outside locations around most campuses. In an emergency, a student can pick up one of these phones (free of charge) to connect with campus police or a security escort.

Campus Police – Police who are specifically assigned to a given institution. Campus police are typically not regular city officers; they are employed by the university in a full-time capacity.

Club Sports – A level of sports that falls somewhere between varsity and intramural. If a student is unable to commit to a varsity team but has a lot of passion for athletics, a club sport could be a better, less intense option. Even less demanding, intramural (IM) sports often involve no traveling and considerably less time.

Cocaine – An illegal drug. Also known as "coke" or "blow," cocaine often resembles a white crystalline or powdery substance. It is highly addictive and dangerous.

Common Application – An application with which students can apply to multiple schools.

Course Registration – The period of official class selection for the upcoming quarter or semester. Prior to registration, it is best to prepare several back-up courses in case a particular class becomes full. If a course is full, students can place themselves on the waitlist, although this still does not guarantee entry.

Division Athletics – Athletic classifications range from Division I to Division III. Division IA is the most competitive, while Division III is considered to be the least competitive.

Dorm – A dorm (or dormitory) is an on-campus housing facility. Dorms can provide a range of options from suite-style rooms to more communal options that include shared bathrooms. Most first-year students live in dorms. Some upperclassmen who wish to stay on campus also choose this option.

Early Action – An application option with which a student can apply to a school and receive an early acceptance response without a binding commitment. This system is becoming less and less available.

Early Decision – An application option that students should use only if they are certain they plan to attend the school in question. If a student applies using the early decision option and is admitted, he or she is required and bound to attend that university. Admission rates are usually higher among students who apply through early decision, as the student is clearly indicating that the school is his or her first choice.

Ecstasy – An illegal drug. Also known as "E" or "X," ecstasy looks like a pill and most resembles an aspirin. Considered a party drug, ecstasy is very dangerous and can be deadly.

Ethernet – An extremely fast Internet connection available in most university-owned residence halls. To use an Ethernet connection properly, a student will need a network card and cable for his or her computer.

Fake ID – A counterfeit identification card that contains false information. Most commonly, students get fake IDs with altered birthdates so that they appear to be older than 21 (and therefore of legal drinking age). Even though it is illegal, many college students have fake IDs in hopes of purchasing alcohol or getting into bars.

Frosh – Slang for "freshman" or "freshmen."

Hazing – Initiation rituals administered by some fraternities or sororities as part of the pledging process. Many universities have outlawed hazing due to its degrading, and sometimes dangerous, nature.

Intramurals (IMs) – A popular, and usually free, sport league in which students create teams and compete against one another. These sports vary in competitiveness and can include a range of activities—everything from billiards to water polo. IM sports are a great way to meet people with similar interests.

Keg – Officially called a half-barrel, a keg contains roughly 200 12-ounce servings of beer.

LSD – An illegal drug, also known as acid, this hallucinogenic drug most commonly resembles a tab of paper.

Marijuana – An illegal drug, also known as weed or pot; along with alcohol, marijuana is one of the most commonly-found drugs on campuses across the country.

Major –The focal point of a student's college studies; a specific topic that is studied for a degree. Examples of majors include physics, English, history, computer science, economics, business, and music. Many students decide on a specific major before arriving on campus, while others are simply "undecided" until declaring a major. Those who are extremely interested in two areas can also choose to double major.

Meal Block – The equivalent of one meal. Students on a meal plan usually receive a fixed number of meals per week. Each meal, or "block," can be redeemed at the school's dining facilities in place of cash. Often, a student's weekly allotment of meal blocks will be forfeited if not used.

Minor – An additional focal point in a student's education. Often serving as a complement or addition to a student's main area of focus, a minor has fewer requirements and prerequisites to fulfill than a major. Minors are not required for graduation from most schools; however some students who want to explore many different interests choose to pursue both a major and a minor.

Mushrooms – An illegal drug. Also known as "'shrooms," this drug resembles regular mushrooms but is extremely hallucinogenic.

Off-Campus Housing – Housing from a particular landlord or rental group that is not affiliated with the university. Depending on the college, off-campus housing can range from extremely popular to non-existent. Students who choose to live off campus are typically given more freedom, but they also have to deal with possible subletting scenarios, furniture, bills, and other issues. In addition to these factors, rental prices and distance often affect a student's decision to move off campus.

Office Hours – Time that teachers set aside for students who have questions about coursework. Office hours are a good forum for students to go over any problems and to show interest in the subject material.

Pledging – The early phase of joining a fraternity or sorority, pledging takes place after a student has gone through rush and received a bid. Pledging usually lasts between one and two semesters. Once the pledging period is complete and a particular student has done everything that is required to become a member, that student is considered a brother or sister. If a fraternity or a sorority would decide to "haze" a group of students, this initiation would take place during the pledging period.

Private Institution – A school that does not use tax revenue to subsidize education costs. Private schools typically cost more than public schools and are usually smaller.

Prof – Slang for "professor."

Public Institution – A school that uses tax revenue to subsidize education costs. Public schools are often a good value for in-state residents and tend to be larger than most private colleges.

Quarter System (or Trimester System) – A type of academic calendar system. In this setup, students take classes for three academic periods. The first quarter usually starts in late September or early October and concludes right before Christmas. The second quarter usually starts around early to mid–January and finishes up around March or April. The last academic quarter, or "third quarter," usually starts in late March or early April and finishes up in late May or Mid-June. The fourth quarter is summer. The major difference between the quarter system and semester system is that students take more, less comprehensive courses under the quarter calendar.

RA (Resident Assistant) – A student leader who is assigned to a particular floor in a dormitory in order to help to the other students who live there. An RA's duties include ensuring student safety and providing assistance wherever possible.

Recitation – An extension of a specific course; a review session. Some classes, particularly large lectures, are supplemented with mandatory recitation sessions that provide a relatively personal class setting.

Rolling Admissions – A form of admissions. Most commonly found at public institutions, schools with this type of policy continue to accept students throughout the year until their class sizes are met. For example, some schools begin accepting students as early as December and will continue to do so until April or May.

Room and Board – This figure is typically the combined cost of a university-owned room and a meal plan.

Room Draw/Housing Lottery – A common way to pick on-campus room assignments for the following year. If a student decides to remain in university-owned housing, he or she is assigned a unique number that, along with seniority, is used to determine his or her housing for the next year.

Rush – The period in which students can meet the brothers and sisters of a particular chapter and find out if a given fraternity or sorority is right for them. Rushing a fraternity or a sorority is not a requirement at any school. The goal of rush is to give students who are serious about pledging a feel for what to expect.

Semester System – The most common type of academic calendar system at college campuses. This setup typically includes two semesters in a given school year. The fall semester starts around the end of August or early September and concludes before winter vacation. The spring semester usually starts in mid-January and ends in late April or May.

Student Center/Rec Center/Student Union – A common area on campus that often contains study areas, recreation facilities, and eateries. This building is often a good place to meet up with fellow students; depending on the school, the student center can have a huge role or a non-existent role in campus life.

Student ID – A university-issued photo ID that serves as a student's key to school-related functions. Some schools require students to show these cards in order to get into dorms, libraries, cafeterias, and other facilities. In addition to storing meal plan information, in some cases, a student ID can actually work as a debit card and allow students to purchase things from bookstores or local shops.

Suite – A type of dorm room. Unlike dorms that feature communal bathrooms shared by the entire floor, suites offer bathrooms shared only among the suite. Suite-style dorm rooms can house anywhere from two to ten students.

TA (Teacher's Assistant) – An undergraduate or grad student who helps in some manner with a specific course. In some cases, a TA will teach a class, assist a professor, grade assignments, or conduct office hours.

Undergraduate – A student in the process of studying for his or her bachelor's degree.

ABOUT THE AUTHOR

When the opportunity to write this guidebook first entered my summer plans, it presented the irresistible charm that every worthwhile challenge does. I found myself drawn to it and yet, dreading the work; so of course, I had to accept it. From that moment on, this project has directed the course of eight weeks of my life—altered plans, created stress, and if you know me, caused shaking. Through all the ups and downs, it has challenged me as a writer, forced me to scrutinize the place I call home eight months of the year, and overall, has been a thoroughly rewarding experience.

I hope this book is revealing and useful in your search for the right college. Now a junior at PC, I know without a doubt this is where I belong, studying English and minoring in history. I look forward to sharpening my writing skills as World News Editor on *The Cowl* and wish to pursue more publishing opportunities in the future. A native of Long Island, NY, I am eager to return to PC to begin my second year as an RA.

There are so many people that I must thank for their love, support, and help during this project: my family for putting up with my cranky, dramatic self when things get stressful; Neil—without whom I would never have gotten any surveys done—for his enthusiasm in utilizing his numerous contacts; to my girls Karen, Monica, Siobhan, Krissy, Meg—you are the champagne bubbles in my life, gabbing, giggling, and gossiping with you make my days, weeks, months, and years; to my friend, the Yale crew-rowing gymnast and microeconomist (wink, wink), the person who by far makes me laugh more than anyone else; to all my friends (new and old, from Kellenberg, PC, and all the places in between), you are the ones who make my daily existence extraordinary— thank you for that; to Tarra for forcing me to take a much needed two-day vacation that ended up being one of the best weekends of the summer. I cannot forget to express my gratitude to Mrs. Von and Mr. Huggard for their continual literary inspiration. And lastly, to everyone at College Prowler for extending this opportunity to me, thank you.

Kathryn Treadway
kathryntreadway@collegeprowler.com

The College Prowler Big Book of Colleges

Having Trouble Narrowing Down Your Choices?

Try Going Bigger!

BIG BOOK OF COLLEGES '09
7¼" X 10", 1248 Pages Paperback
$29.95 Retail
978-1-4274-0005-5

Choosing the perfect school can be an overwhelming challenge. Luckily, our *Big Book of Colleges* makes that task a little less daunting. We've packed it with overviews of our full library of single-school guides—more than 280 of the nation's top schools—giving you some much-needed perspective on your search.

College Prowler
on the Web

Get the Jolt!

College Jolt gives you a peek behind the scenes

College Jolt is our new blog designed to hook you up with great information, funny videos, cool contests, awesome scholarship opportunities, and honest insight into who we are and what we're all about.

Check us out at ***www.collegejolt.com***

Tell Us What Life Is Really Like at Your School!

Have you ever wanted to let people know what your college is really like? Now's your chance to help millions of high school students choose the right college.

Let your voice be heard.

Check out *www.collegeprowler.com* for more info!

Need More Help?

Do you have more questions about this school? Can't find a certain statistic? College Prowler is here to help. We are the best source of college information out there. We have a network of thousands of students who can get the latest information on any school to you ASAP. E-mail us at info@collegeprowler.com with your college-related questions.

E-Mail Us Your College-Related Questions!

Check out **www.collegeprowler.com** for more details.
1-800-290-2682

Write For Us!
Get published! Voice your opinion.

Writing a College Prowler guidebook is both fun and rewarding; our open-ended format allows your own creativity free reign. Our writers have been featured in national newspapers and have seen their names in bookstores across the country. Now is your chance to break into the publishing industry with one of the country's fastest-growing publishers!

Apply now at **www.collegeprowler.com**

Contact editor@collegeprowler.com or call 1-800-290-2682 for more details.

Pros and Cons

Still can't figure out if this is the right school for you?
You've already read through this in-depth guide;
why not list the pros and cons? It will really help
with narrowing down your decision and determining
whether or not this school is right for you.

Pros	Cons
....	....
....	....
....	....
....	....
....	....
....	....
....	....
....	....
....	....
....	....
....	....
....	....
....	....

Pros and Cons

Still can't figure out if this is the right school for you?
You've already read through this in-depth guide;
why not list the pros and cons? It will really help
with narrowing down your decision and determining
whether or not this school is right for you.

Pros	**Cons**
....	....
....	....
....	....
....	....
....	....
....	....
....	....
....	....
....	....
....	....
....	....
....	....
....	....

Notes

....

....

....

....

....

....

....

....

....

....

....

....

....

....

Notes

....
....
....
....
....
....
....
....
....
....
....
....
....

Notes

....

....

....

....

....

....

....

....

....

....

....

....

....

Notes

....

....

....

....

....

....

....

....

....

....

....

....

....

Notes

Notes

....
....
....
....
....
....
....
....
....
....
....
....
....

Notes

....

....

....

....

....

....

....

....

....

....

....

....

....

Notes

....

....

....

....

....

....

....

....

....

....

....

....

....

Notes

....

....

....

....

....

....

....

....

....

....

....

....

....

Notes

....

....

....

....

....

....

....

....

....

....

....

....

....

Notes

....

....

....

....

....

....

....

....

....

....

....

....

....

Notes

Notes

....
....
....
....
....
....
....
....
....
....
....
....
....

Notes

Notes

....

....

....

....

....

....

....

....

....

....

....

....

....

Notes

....

....

....

....

....

....

....

....

....

....

....

....

....

Notes

....

....

....

....

....

....

....

....

....

....

....

....

....

Notes

....

....

....

....

....

....

....

....

....

....

....

....

....

Notes

....

....

....

....

....

....

....

....

....

....

....

....

....

Notes

....

....

....

....

....

....

....

....

....

....

....

....

....

....

Notes

....

....

....

....

....

....

....

....

....

....

....

....

....

Notes

....

....

....

....

....

....

....

....

....

....

....

....

....

Notes

....

....

....

....

....

....

....

....

....

....

....

....

....

Notes

Notes

....

....

....

....

....

....

....

....

....

....

....

....

....

....

Notes

....

....

....

....

....

....

....

....

....

....

....

....

....

....

Notes

....

....

....

....

....

....

....

....

....

....

....

....

....

LaVergne, TN USA
16 December 2010
208997LV00007B/1/P